PANCAKE

Edible

Series Editor: Andrew F. Smith

EDIBLE is a revolutionary new series of books dedicated to food and drink that explores the rich history of cuisine. Each book reveals the global history and culture of one type of food or beverage.

Already published

Hamburger Andrew F. Smith

Pizza Carol Helstosky

Forthcoming

Spices Fred Czarra

Pie Janet Clarkson

Beer Peter La France

Cake Nicola Humble

Caviar Nicola Fletcher

Chocolate Sarah Moss

Cocktails Joseph M. Carlin

Curry Colleen Taylor Sen

Fish and Chips Panikos Panayi

Hot Dog Bruce Kraig

Lobster Elisabeth Townsend

Tea Helen Saberi

Tomato Deborah A. Duchon

Pancake

A Global History

Ken Albala

REAKTION BOOKS

Published by Reaktion Books Ltd
33 Great Sutton Street
London EC1V 0DX
www.reaktionbooks.co.uk

First published 2008

Printed and bound in China by C&C Offset Printing Co., Ltd

British Library Cataloguing in Publication Data
Albala, Ken, 1964–
Pancake : a global history. – (Edible)
1. Pancakes, waffles, etc. 2. Pancakes, waffles, etc. –
History
I. Title
641.8'15

ISBN-13: 978 1 86189 392 5

Contents

Introduction:
What is a Pancake?

A pancake is a starch-based comestible, poured as a batter onto a hot surface and cooked until solid. Normally round and formed by force of gravity, pancakes can also be cooked in a mould or drizzled into any number of free-form shapes. They are usually, and proverbially, flat, though with the right ingredients an adept hand can create light fluffy specimens that rise in defiance of the horizon. On the other hand, a slim figure is consciously sought for many types, as with the French crêpe. Pancakes can be minuscule, 'silver dollar' size or great heaped behemoths of batter – the sort made for charity benefits, or by those hoping for a spot in the *Guinness World Records*. Pancakes may be made at home, eaten at a restaurant or bought from a street vendor.

We all know a pancake when we see one, but appearances can be deceptive. To the untrained eye, a flat pitta bread or corn tortilla bears close affinity to the pancake. Yet a fundamental distinction must be made: all these starchy staples may have evolved in comparable ways from similar ingredients, but they are in fact unrelated. They are as remote as hummingbirds and bumblebees or sharks and dolphins. Though they can be used in comparable ways, folded or wrapped around fillings, pancakes are always made from a

Simple fluffy pancakes are a classic breakfast food in the US.

poured batter rather than rolled dough. Flat bread is precisely
that – comparatively stiff dough worked manually and then
baked in an oven or on a flat surface. Even though minimally
leavened and looking much like a pancake, it is still a form of
bread. Furthermore, not all items calling themselves pancakes
truly fit the description – the Chinese *po-ping* that cradles
Peking duck or *moo-shu* pork is a thin rolled flat bread; South
East Asian rice wrappers used to make spring rolls are more
a kind of noodle, dried and reconstituted with water.

Leavening agents are used in most pancakes, but are not
an essential part of their definition. Pancakes can rise with
the aid of baking powder or soda, or may feature yeast, car-
bonated water, beaten egg white – or no leavening at all.
Though pancakes normally have at least a certain suggestion
of aeration in the finished product, flour and water alone
can be enough. The ancestors of pancakes were leavened
mostly by the incorporation of air into the batter, expanding
when heated. In the UK this is still the preferred method. Of

all the remarkable leavening agents, none is as arresting as snow. In *Miss Parloa's New Cookbook* (1881), it is mixed into an apple-laden batter at the last minute, and then dropped into boiling fat – perhaps producing something more like a fritter, but called a snow pancake.

The range of ingredients used plays no part in the essential definition of the pancake. Pitta and pancakes can both be made from the same flour, moistened in varying degrees. Yet a perfectly respectable pancake can be made without using any wheat flour at all. Grains in general cannot claim exclusive dominion over the pancake. While barley, rice and corn, even buckwheat, have all made their contribution to pancakes, so too have chestnuts and acorns, leguminous seeds pounded into flour. Indeed, any form of starch can and has been used to make pancakes through the annals of history. Some nineteenth-century American pancakes were even made with stale breadcrumbs. It is not what goes into the bowl that defines the pancake, but what comes out of the pan.

Cooking technology plays a decisive role in separating pancakes from what are otherwise close relatives. Pancakes are by definition cooked or, to employ the proper terminology, baked in a pan, though any flat surface will suffice. Indeed, mass-produced pancakes are almost always cooked on a broad griddle or professional flat top, to leave the batter unfettered by the constricting rim of a domestic frying pan. A flat stone moistened with grease and placed over burning embers may have held the ur-pancake of our prehistoric ancestors. Thus a pan does not the pancake make. And neither can the range of ridged and coffered confections designed to ravish the devotees of waffledom be justly inscribed in our paean to pure panned cake. Moreover, for purposes of clarification, by cooking pancakes we denote specifically the application of direct heat with a modicum of grease of animal or vegetable origin, and not deep frying which produces an entirely different product, though composed of much the same ingredients. Fritters are made of pancake batter, as are funnel cakes (literally poured through a funnel into hot fat creating a randomly drizzled pattern), but they are not pancakes. As we shall see, however, in the past a crunchy fried fritter was often called a pancake.

Moreover, the exact ingredients used to make pancakes may, through different cooking procedures, yield products we would never consider part of the same family. Consider for a moment the whole range of dumplings: German *spaetzle*, potato gnocchi, and the ancestral puddings of Britain – sometimes nothing more than pancake batter boiled in a stomach bag with suet and raisins. These have a closer affinity to pancakes than do most flat breads.

Another distinction must be made with the variety of soufflé known as Yorkshire pudding, or in the US, popovers, which is made with a batter very similar to that of the pancake, but usually with a greater proportion of eggs. This is always baked in a mould to achieve supreme puffiness rather than the flatness of a pancake. Yorkshire pudding anointed by drippings, and the perversely named 'Dutch Baby' or German pancakes (Dutch here meaning Deutsch) must be set aside. On the other hand, there are many varieties of pancake with a great proportion of beaten egg whites that come very close to being popovers. And some 'pancakes' are so overburdened with egg that they are more like omelettes tousled with flour for effect. Here we mince words, if not ingredients.

Is the pancake truly a cake? It is not as we envision cake today – a fluffy confection, baked in an oven and often slathered with icing. At heart, however, by archaic English

Waffles, despite their eminent popularity, are not pancakes.

usage and even by constituent ingredients, the pancake is closely related to all other cakes. Ontogeny recapitulates phylogeny or, more plainly put, the evolution of a species can be discerned in its developing embryonic state. The pancake might be considered a primitive prototype of all cakes. Observe the pancake in the process of formation: sifted dry flour, a drizzle of milk, beaten eggs, a little sugar, perhaps a leavening. What is the wedding cake but a sublimation of this simple procedure after it had evolved under the influence of advanced technology? Behold the towering pancake stack, glimmering with syrup, and it requires little imagination to recognize that this is truly a kind of cake.

More difficult to define, however, is the group of cakes formed from neither wet batter nor stiff bread dough: crumpets, muffins, as well as quick breads, corn breads and beaten biscuits – these may be comely, but they are not proper pancakes. The great Scots bannock, oaten farl and Oban crowdie bear rudiments of common ancestry, but should never be confounded with the pancake. Distinctively sweet and tiny, Scots pancakes, known outside their native highlands as drop scones, are indeed little pancakes. As are New Zealand pikelets, not teeny fish, but Lilliputian pancakes.

Thus far we have defined the pancake in decidedly Eurocentric terms as a flat batter-based cake cooked in a pan or similar vessel, with or without leavening, and made from any starchy base. The last of these qualifications gives rise to a troop of relatives we would probably not expect to find in a standard greasy spoon. Many of us are intimately acquainted with the potato pancake or latke – a central feature of Hanukkah festivities. When the potato is grated, formed into cakes and fried, the result is merely a hash brown, but there also exists a variety blended into a smooth batter and poured out precisely as other pancakes, differing only in size and texture. We must recognize the basic affinity and shared nomenclature in this case and afford the latke some coverage. The same goes for the Swedish *raggmunk*, a regular pancake bolstered with shredded potatoes. So too must we include the African bean cake *akara* and its New World siblings, made with batter and akin to the latke in texture and character. And then why not welcome into our pancake ranks the *socca*, a chickpea cake of southern France, sometimes baked but often cooked on a special flat griddle regularly used for crêpes?

There should be no quibble in adding to our taxonomic list various other well-recognized relatives: crêpes themselves (though etymologically and originally 'crisps') as well as the buckwheat Breton galette, Russian blini, the rotund Scandinavian *aebleskiver* and *plättar*, not to mention the Hungarian *palacsinta*. Nor can we omit more far-flung cousins, the great teff-based *injera* of Ethiopia, the resplendent rice and bean *dosa* of southern India, the corn *cachapa* of Venezuela,

Akara are African pancakes made from black-eyed peas.

Japanese *okonomiyaki*, sweet *dorayaki* and Thai *pak moh*. Pancakes, we must keep in mind, can be sweet or savoury, adorned or simple, consumed during any meal and in any setting. Without going out on a limb, it would not be far fetched to claim that, among the myriad recipes and cooking techniques on this planet, there are few that can claim such universality or so noble a pedigree as the pancake.

Despite this enthusiastic and inclusive spirit, there remains one final difficulty in defining the pancake with precision. How are we to classify closely related tribes whose members begin life as pancakes, but are then transformed into something else entirely? The Egyptian *katief*, for example, is a pancake cooked on one side only, filled with nuts or pastry cream, sealed and then deep fried. The Italian *cannoli* must be considered a relative and so too must the cheese-filled blintz. On first sight no one would call these pancakes, though only a brief affair with hot fat separates them from a rolled crêpe. Thus we confine ourselves only to those foods which begin and end as recognizable pancakes.

To reiterate, a pancake is here defined as a flat cake made of any starchy batter, normally cooked in a small amount of fat on a flat surface, with anything from a hint of leavening to positive fluffiness, yet retaining a soft pliable interior structure. Thus close relatives such as crisp fritters, doughnuts and wafers, rolled and fried confections and even the estimable waffle family are excluded.

How should a pancake be made? There are as many answers to that question as there are able cooks and eager mouths to feed. Having spent roughly half a decade in graduate school, patiently making a pancake every single morning without exception, I can offer some hard-won tips. It is possible to use any combination of starch in any proportion – cake flour, wholewheat, cornmeal, buckwheat, rye, chestnut

A Native American woman cooking pancakes outdoors.

flour are all delightful. Even soy flour makes an interesting pancake. For a light texture, avoid using too many eggs. The ideal proportion of ingredients, in my opinion, is 1 egg to 2 cups/250 g of flour and 2 cups/235 ml of milk, with a teaspoon of baking soda. This is a standard American pancake, though you will encounter endless variations of the measures specified in recipes. The great nineteenth-century chef Alexis Soyer, for example, used 4 eggs with a mere 4 small tablespoons of flour, two tablespoons of sugar and a pint/470 ml of milk. This would pass as an omelette in most people's minds, although it is typical of eighteenth- and nineteenth-century pancake recipes.

Thickness, on the other hand, is purely a matter of personal and sometimes national predilection. If you prefer thinner pancakes, use more milk. If you only need one big pancake, use just the egg white and 1 cup/125 g of flour with enough milk to make a thick batter. You can also use

Children are mesmerized by bright colours suspended in the pancake batter.

buttermilk or add a little yoghurt to the mix – the acidity helps the baking powder work. Sour milk was used in the past but, since the advent of mandatory pasteurization in many countries, milk only rots; it doesn't properly sour from beneficial bacteria. Some pancake recipes include fat in the batter – normally melted butter – but I contend that it is much better on top of the hot stack or excluded altogether, otherwise the pancake runs the risk of becoming cloying. In place of dairy products one can use water, wine or theoretically any liquid. Sugar in the batter is also an option, but tends to make the pancake heavier and more prone to burning. Flavourings such as vanilla extract or almond are fine; even rosewater perks up a plaintive pancake. Food colouring can also be fun: try a couple of drops of various hues once the batter hits the pan, and then swirl them around with a toothpick to create a lovely marbling effect.

As for inclusions, anything goes. But rather than dump ingredients into the batter and then risk their scorching from direct contact with the pan, it is preferable to pour the batter first and then drop the berries or chocolate chips, or whatever, on top. Then gently submerge them into the molten batter with the tip of a knife so they are completely covered. Without this simple step, blueberries explode and stain the pancake, making a hideous mess. Chocolate chips likewise

Blueberry pancakes are best with berries submerged in the batter. Here they peer through unscathed.

stick to the pan. For savoury ingredients, this step is less important. Shredded spring onions or chives benefit from the direct heat and decorate the finished product. For the adventurous palate, anything can be thrown in: nuts, leftover vegetables, grated cheese, smoked salmon or bacon. All these can be cooked in the batter or sealed in the rolled or folded pancake after cooking. Just be sure not to load too much into the batter lest it resist cohesion while cooking.

As for the cooking medium, butter is ideal, but one should never use more than a smidgen to prevent sticking, or the pancake comes out greasy. Oil also works, as does lard or bacon grease. Duck fat yields remarkable results, preferably with savoury pancakes. Non-stick pans allow you to use less fat, but are rarely really good conductors of heat. Cast iron is lovely, but makes flipping nearly impossible. But then, few pancakes truly benefit from a toss in the air and some will actually splatter; a gentle turn with a spatula is fine. Some contend that a pancake should never be turned more than once, but this must be pure superstition. This next suggestion may sound absurdly fastidious, but it really does improve practically any pancake. If you are making several pancakes and need to keep them warm, haphazard stacking causes the ambient steam of those freshly cooked to seep into the others, making them all soggy. Try placing the fresh pancakes on a rack in a warm oven. Even the solitary pancake is better for spending a brief sojourn on a raised rack so the steam can dissipate. I have even been seen waving my pancake in the air for a moment before plopping it on a plate.

Of all the pancakes I have ever made or eaten, there is one favourite – unconventional admittedly, related to a soufflé and fairly complicated – that is well worth the effort and which I humbly encourage readers to try. I have a pathological aversion to measurements, so one must succumb to inexactness here and allow one's inner pancake to speak through the basic procedure. A runnier batter naturally makes thinner cakes; this batter should be so thick and so inflated that it must be scooped gently from the bowl with a rubber spatula.

Panned-Cake (Enough for One Person)

Begin with one egg yolk in a capacious bowl and beat until pale and thickened with a spoonful of unrefined sugar. Add to the beaten yolk a few drops of pure vanilla extract. Next, sift over some cake flour, less than a cupful. Add a scant teaspoon of baking powder and a tiny pinch of salt into the sieve as well as a dusting of freshly grated nutmeg. Then, with a clean whisk beat the egg white in a second bowl with a minuscule fleck of cream of tartar until quite stiff. Then add to the yolk and dry ingredients a good pour of buttermilk (or regular milk) and stir until it forms a thick batter. Do not over-mix. Then gently fold in the beaten egg white. Melt a little butter over a high heat in a non-stick frying pan, then carefully place a good gob of the batter mixture into the pan. Lower the flame and leave undisturbed until little craters start forming on the surface. Allow the cake to rise. Flipping in air is not recommended here as it reduces the aeration and the batter will definitely splatter; gently turn over with a wide spatula instead. Serve hot one at a time with real amber maple syrup on the side in a small dipping bowl. And eat it with your fingers. Or just dust with powdered sugar, cinnamon, cocoa powder, whatever.

A Pancake is Born

We may speculate with the archaeologist regarding the earliest culinary technologies available at the dawn of humanity. Roasting, in a pit or before an open flame, surely came first. Boiling in baskets holding water heated with stones from the fire probably followed suit. But among these too must be the primeval griddle, perhaps a flat rock, daubed with grease and glistening in anticipation of the first dollop of Promethean batter. Any primitive grain or tuber, dried, pounded and moistened, could have given rise to the very first pancake. With the domestication of wheat in the Fertile Crescent, corn in the Americas and rice in Asia, not to mention the countless other starchy staples cultivated around the globe, the pancake would find expression in countless forms. One can almost envision the weary Neolithic farmer's wife, wracking her brains to introduce variety to her family's meagre daily sustenance. In a flash of insight she pours a blob from the dreary pot of gruel onto a brazen shield resting over the fire, resulting in a crisp yet pliable disc, fluffy and evanescent, yet substantial and filling: the prototype of every civilized pancake in its wake.

Soon it was discovered that these discs could be used to mop up thick sauces, and thereafter were wrapped around savoury titbits both to protect the fingers and to convey the contents to the mouth. These tidy packages also proved portable, and an early form of rolled crêpe was sold on the bustling street corners of the most ancient villages and towns. Furthermore, ingredients could be directly incorporated into the batter, blueberries being classic, but elsewhere onions or dried shrimp, pork, indeed anything that could be encased in batter. Because they were cheap and nourishing, pancakes sustained the labourers who toiled over the

Rembrandt's famous 17th-century evocation of pancake cookery.

construction of great monuments; chefs of the rich and powerful concocted ever-new ways to entice the palate with elegant pancake concoctions. From the humblest cottage to the grandest palace, pancakes became one of the premier comfort foods, beloved by children and relished into adult-hood as a simply prepared but eminently elegant repast.

Strangely enough though, historic recipes for pancakes are few and far between. This is probably because for most of recorded history recipes have only been written down when ingredients are expensive or procedures complex. The word pancake did not appear until the late middle ages, and even then a 'pancake' was not always a pancake.

The records of history do not, alas, record the first pancake, or even its earliest forms. Ancient authors meticulously recorded many flattish cakes, such as libum, used in sacrifice by the Romans. Even the ancient Hebrews served the Lord a form of pancake. In Chronicles 23:29 the Levites are given responsibility for the bread offerings, fried pastries and 'that which is baked in the pan'. Among their cakes, the Greeks had a flat cake known as *plakous*, which actually means flat and which came to be known in Latin strangely enough as 'placenta' (from Greek *plakounta* in the accusative). The modern anatomical use of the term derives from its resemblance to the original pancake form. Some of these cakes were almost certainly cooked in ways that to our sensibilities must be types of pancake, but in general they are more closely related to what we think of as a cheesecake, containing honey, cheese and flour. The Greeks also had something called *tagênitai* among the Athenians, or *têganitai* among the Greeks of Asia Minor. Both come from the Greek word *tegano*, meaning frying pan, so their literal meaning is pancakes. They are mentioned by the physician Galen in *Alimentorum facultatibus*, and appear to be just a flour and water batter (or perhaps a dough) fried in oil and turned a few times. Some mix in honey or oil, he adds. Interestingly, his association is with country folk or very poor townsfolk, who make flat cakes from whatever is at hand. All these,

Galen insists, restrain the stomach and create thick juice (by which he means nutritive substance) which converts into crude humours. In other words, they are fairly indigestible. Although he provides no recipe, so we cannot be sure, these appear to be among the earliest of pancakes. That some were indeed poured from a batter is evident in his calling some types of cake 'pour-cakes'.

There was another kind of flat-dough product called *laganum*. There is disagreement among modern commentators over its identity, taken by some to be an ancestor of lasagne (to which it is related etymologically), though not boiled. It was probably a kind of dried flat dough, although in later centuries the word was translated as pancake. What it was originally, no one is absolutely certain. In the English–Latin dictionary, *Catholicon Anglicum* of 1483, pancake is translated as *opacum* or *laganum*. The true identity of the word *opacum* is also a mystery, though it is somehow related to the word for shady or opaque. The name and shape suggests that it may have been something that resembled an umbrella, but that's only a guess. In any case, only medieval Europeans, and not the ancients, used these terms for pancake.

There is a recipe in the oldest Latin cookbook attributed to Apicius for *ova sfongia ex lacte* (egg sponge with milk) which comes close to a modern pancake. It is made with 4 eggs, a *hemina* of milk (½ pint/240 ml) and an ounce/30 ml of oil. This batter is fried in a thin pan with a little heated oil. When one side is done, it's flipped and served with pepper and honey. This contains no flour and is clearly a spongy omelette as the recipe says, not a pancake. Furthermore, though some modern authors contend that pancakes were known in Apicius as 'alita dolcia', meaning another sweet, this recipe is really just fried polenta with honey on top, and nothing like a pancake. The very first pancake-like recipe is found in the middle ages, and is none other than the French crêpe. But this word did not mean what it later came to signify – a large thin and floppy pancake. Remarkably, the word itself descends from the word for crisp, and is related to older forms of crisp fritter which in Latin were known as *crispis* (meaning curly, which these first crisps probably were). In Italian these became known as *crispelli* or *crespelle*, the latter of which still survive, though like crêpes they began as deep-fried fritters and only later became thin pancakes.

The first crêpe recipe is not recorded in the courtly cookbooks of medieval France, probably because crêpes were considered lowly fare for ordinary people, which is also probably why they show up in the book of advice written by an ageing city dweller for his young bride in *Le Menagier de Paris*. In fact there are two crêpe recipes. The first is merely a simple mixture of flour, eggs, water, salt and wine. This is beaten up and then poured from a bowl with a hole in the bottom, which must have been designed especially for this recipe, into a pan of hot lard or lard and butter. It is served with powdered sugar. The technique and the fact that a deep pan with straight sides is called for suggests that these are neither pancakes nor modern crêpes, but crispy funnel cakes. The slightly more complicated recipe for 'Crespes a la Guise de Tournay', which clearly shows a long-perfected technique, confirms this:

> First you must have ready a copper pan holding a quart, of which the rim must not be wider than the base, or just a bit, and let it be 4 or 3½ fingers deep. Take salted butter and melt, skimming and cleaning, then pour into another pan leaving all the solids behind, and add the same amount of good fresh

lard. Then crack eggs and remove half the whites, and the remaining ones beat well with both whites and yolks. Then take a third or quarter of white wine and mix all together. Then take the most beautiful wheat flour you can get, and beat together little by little, as long as will tire one or two people, and your batter should be neither thin nor thick, but such as can pour easily through a hole the size of a little finger. Then put your butter and your lard on the fire together, as much of one as the other, so that it boils, then take your batter and fill a bowl or a big wooden ladle with a hole, and pour into your grease, first in the middle of the pan, then turning to the edges of your pan until full. Always beat your batter without stopping, to make other crêpes. And this crêpe which is in the pan can be lifted with a skewer or stick, and turn over to cook, then remove, put on a plate, and begin with another. Be sure always to stir and beat the batter without stopping.

Although this recipe can be used to make what we would recognize as a pancake, it still seems likely that in wealthier households a few inches of fat would have been used, yielding a fritter. More modest abodes, without the wherewithal to use large amounts of fat for deep frying, are probably the origin of true pancakes. Similar confections appear in other medieval manuscripts, including a kind of wafer, or *obelias*, and *mistembec*, although these were normally made in a kind of long-handled waffle iron. We must surmise that the medieval crêpes, being called crisps, were supposed to be crisp, to some degree. A contemporary Latin manuscript written in Italy, the *Liber de coquina*, for example, offers a simple recipe ('De crispis'): Take white flour moistened with hot

Jules Benoit-Lévy's depiction of a traditional Breton tavern where pancakes were sold.

water and fermented with yeast so that it rises. And cook in a pan with bubbling oil. And add honey, and eat. Following it are 'crispellas' which include eggs and saffron rather than yeast. All these are indeed very close relatives to the floppy pancake, but how and when they were first cooked in a small amount of oil, not bubbling and no longer becoming crisp, is anyone's guess. The development of pancakes probably did not take place in southern Europe, where deep-frying fritters in countless forms remained all the rage from the late Middle Ages to the early modern period.

The first example of the modern crêpe in print might be the recipe found in the *Livre fort excellent* of the 1540s in which 'crespes faictes en poelle' are made from a simple batter of fine flour, white wine and egg whites cooked in clarified butter. Since this cookbook seems to address a fairly popular bourgeois audience, it may be the cheap affordable crêpe alluded to above, though the amount of butter used is not specified.

Although often cited as the first pancake recipe in English, the Harleian Ms. 279 actually contains only the first use of the word in a cookery book; the recipe itself is for 'Towres', made of egg yolk and marrow, spices and perhaps chopped pork or veal if you like. The white of the egg is strained and then fried like a pancake: 'þan putte a litel of þe Whyte comade in þe panne, & late flete al a-brode as þou makyst a pancake'. Then the yolk mixture goes on top and the round edges are folded in to form a square. So it is actually an omelette variation. The manuscript includes many pancake-like recipes though, including the medieval ancestor of the crêpe, here called 'Cryspe' – which it is, since it is basically a pancake batter (egg whites, milk, flour and yeast, sugar and salt) drizzled by hand (the batter runs through your fingers) into hot fat and removed with a skimmer, letting the fat drain off. Not exactly a pancake; again, more like a funnel cake, or the fritters mentioned above. In conclusion, there are not really any pancake recipes from the Middle Ages, but that doesn't mean that people weren't cooking and eating them.

It is not until the early modern period that true pancake recipes begin to abound, in northern Europe in particular. *A Proper Newe Booke of Cokerye* has many fritter-like concoctions, but nothing for pancakes, even though in the recipe for 'vautes' we are directed to take the eggs and 'frye them as thynne as a pancake' (fo. Bii). On top of this go veal kidney, egg yolks, dates, raisins and spices. Interestingly, the word 'vautes' survives in north-eastern France, where it means crêpe in Lorraine and Ardenne.

Good Huswifes Handmaide for the Kitchen of 1588 has the first recipe in English for a proper pancake, perhaps the first in print anywhere. The mere thumb-sized bit of butter and pan-tilting technique plainly reveal that this is not a deep-fried fritter. On the other hand, it is extraordinarily rich and quite unlike any pancake with which modern readers are likely to be familiar. Unfortunately, if the directions are followed precisely, the result is a horrible mess. With the prescribed proportions, rather more than the suggested one handful of flour is necessary to make a batter that will hold together. One can only imagine that the author was either careless or had gargantuan hands. With enough flour to make a thin batter, this recipe results in a lacy, obscenely rich and very soft pancake with delightfully crisp edges. But eating more than one is out of the question:

To make Pancakes

Take new thicke Creame a pinte, foure or five yolks of Egs, a good handfull of flower, and two or three spoonfuls of Ale, strain them altogether into a faire platter, and season it with a good handfull of Sugar, a spoonful of Synamon, and a litle Ginger: then take a frying pan, and put in a litle peece of Butter, as big as your thombe, and when it is molten browne, cast it out of your pan, and with a ladle put to the further saide of your pan some of your stuffe, and hold your pan aslope, so that your stuffe may run abroad over all your pan, as thin as may be: then set it to the fyre, and let the fyre be verie soft, and when the one side is baked, then turne the other, and bake them as dry as ye can without burning.

In the seventeenth century, Gervase Markham offers a pancake recipe in *The English Housewife* which is aesthetically

Pancakes being cooked in a pan with a long handle over a fire, and being enjoyed by children.

diametrically opposed to the one just cited. The exuberant and even gaudy Elizabethan recipe above, here becomes stark, even a bit puritanical. As Markham insists, it does come out a bit more crisp with just egg and water in the batter, but it is also remarkably dull and ponderous, despite the interesting combination of spices. (Strangely, mixing the two recipes, a culinary *via media*, yields very pleasant results, much like a modern pancake):

The best Pancake

To make the best Pancake, take two or three eggs, and breake them into a dish, and beate them well: Then adde unto them a pretty quantity of faire running water, and beate all well together: Then put in cloves, mace, cinnamon, and a nutmegge, and season it with salt; which done make thicke as you thinke good with fine wheate flower: Then frie the cakes as thinne as may bee with sweet butter, or sweete seame, and make them browne, and so serve them up with sugar strowed upon them. There be some which mixe Pancakes with new milke or creame, but that makes them tough, cloying, and not so crispe, pleasant and savory as running water.

Appropriately, the royalist Robert May begs to differ on the matter of cream. In *The Accomplisht Cook* (1660) in which most lilies are gilded, pancakes require no less than 3 pints of cream, a quart of flour, 8 eggs and 3 nutmegs, plus 2 pounds of clarified butter right in the batter. The effect was indeed intended to be unctuous, especially after then being fried and sprinkled with sugar. It is the epitome of a baroque pancake, if such a thing can be imagined, hurtling through the clouds, held aloft by cherubs. To be fair, he also offers variants using water, or cream and rosewater, though all are heavily spiced too.

Perhaps it would be better to search among the Dutch, indefatigable pancake-eaters, for the earliest recipes. In fact, the oldest Dutch cookbook, *Een Notabel boecxken van cokeryen*,

Adriaen Brouwer, *The Pancake Baker*, mid-1620s, oil on panel.

printed in about 1514, includes 'panckoecken'. These are distinguished from 'struyven', which here definitely refers to fried funnel cakes. The pancakes, suitable for Lent, begin with fine flour beaten up with yeast. From this is made dough, rather than a batter, since a lump of it is made as thin as possible, presumably by rolling, though this is not specified. This is fried, interestingly enough, in rapeseed oil (rather than butter or lard, which would have been forbidden during Lent).

An enthusiastic customer at a Breton crêpe stand.

The 'panckoecken' can be studded with raisins or bits of apple. Despite the name, they seem to be flat breads, unless by a lump the author meant a dollop.

Only in seventeenth-century Netherlands are true pancake recipes to be found, and the Dutch might even lay claim to the invention of the modern pancake. *De Verstandige Kock* has three lovely ones. The simplest is just a pound of wheat flour, a pint of sweet milk and 3 eggs with a little sugar. Groeninger Pancakes are similar but include a pound of currants and some cinnamon and are fried in butter. But to fry the best kind of pancakes (Om de beste slagh van Pannekoecken te maken), 5 or 6 eggs should be beaten with running water (again, because they're tough made with milk or cream) to which are added cloves, cinnamon, mace and nutmeg with some salt, and the best wheat flour. These are cooked and sprinkled with sugar.

They are almost exactly the same as Markham's dull spiced pancakes. The author's first recipe is actually preferable.

To confirm with absolute certainty that these are pancakes rather than crisps, one need only refer to Dutch paintings of the period, especially *A Woman Holding Pancakes* by Jan van Bijlert, painted about the same time as these recipes were written, in the mid-seventeenth century. In it a forlorn woman stares into the distance, with her right hand lifting a delicately thin, almost translucent, pancake from a stack on a pewter plate. Otherwise unadorned, their only accompaniment a small glass of thin red wine. Perhaps, as a zealous art historian would probably point out, the pancake is a symbol of her virginity because, although flexible, it remains unbroken, and the bloodlike wine is not yet spilled. What she contemplates is her impending wedding day, and her Christian duty to be fruitful and multiply. Or maybe it's just a pancake.

The Dutch also developed other pancake forms such as *flensje* – a thin crêpe-like cake made of unleavened dough. There are also pancakes, made in a pan with round depressions, called *poffertjes* or *bollebuisjes* – relatives of the Scandinavian *aebleskiver*. It is sometimes contended that all these forms were transported with Dutch settlers to the New World, in the colony of New Netherlands (now New York) along with other specialities such as cookies and waffles. The Dutch may be the origin of the American pancake craze, but pancakes could just as easily have been imported by the British who, as we have seen, had a form of pancakes in the seventeenth century.

By the eighteenth century, pancakes abound in British cookbooks. E. Smith's *The Compleat Houswife,* also the first cookbook printed in America, includes a recipe using a pint of cream, 8 eggs, a whole grated nutmeg, a little salt and an entire pound of melted butter with a little sack (i.e. sherry). To this is added a mere 3 spoonfuls of flour. The result is an extraordinarily rich and thin omelette sprinkled with sugar, but scarcely resembling a modern pancake. Her recipe for rice pancakes is actually a little closer, but it too is mostly cream and butter thickened with rice and wheat flour.

In an earlier text, Mary Kettilby's *A Collection Above Three Hundred Receipts in Cookery* (1714), there is the delightful conceit of stacking thin pancakes so they resemble a stack or 'quire' of paper. But the minuscule proportion of flour once again results in something quite different from a pancake batter:

> Take to a pint of Cream, eight Eggs, leaving out two whites, three spoonfuls of fine Flower, three spoonfuls of Sack, and some spoonful of Orange-flower-Water, a little Sugar, a grated Nutmeg, and a quarter of a pound of Butter, melted in the cream; mingle all well together, mixing the Flower with a little Cream at first, that it may be smooth: Butter your Pan for the first Pancake and let them run as thin as you can possibly to be whole, when one side is colour'd 'tis enough; take them carefully out of the Pan, and strew some fine sifted Sugar between each; lay them as even on each other as you can: This quantity will make Twenty.

The most popular English cookbook of the century on both sides of the Atlantic, Hannah Glasse's *The Art of Cookery* of 1747, has five proper pancake recipes. They are cooked only with a piece of butter the size of a walnut, and thus not deep-fried, and the author specifies pouring a ladleful of batter into the pan 'which will make a Pancake moving the Pan round, that the Batter be all over the Pan'. They are then either tossed or carefully turned over, again positive proof

Netherlandish pancake cookery, replete with a pot of batter.

that these are the genuine article. Some of Glasse's recipes use only the typical three spoonfuls of flour, but others instruct to add flour until a batter 'of a proper Thickness' forms, and this may be the printed recipe with which American colonists were first familiar. That Charlotte Mason includes a recipe for 'New England Pancakes' among many varieties in *The Lady's Assistant* of 1775 is also a good indication that a

The US encouraged citizens to eat cornmeal during World War I so the government could send wheat, which was considered more nutritious, to soldiers on the front.

separate American pancake tradition was already in place, though there is nothing in the recipe itself that denotes any distinction in form or ingredients.

However they arrived, by the time the first truly American cookbook was printed, Amelia Simmons's appropriately named *American Cookery* (1796), the pancake is centrally featured, in several forms and with a much wider variety of starchy ingredients as well. Using native or alternative ingredients is typical of American pancake recipes for the next century or so. Here is her simple Federal Pan Cake compounded of European and Native stock; Indian meal is corn (maize):

Take one quart of boulted rye flour, one quart of boulted Indian meal, mix it well and stir it with a little salt in three pints of milk, to the proper consistence of pancakes; fry in lard and serve up warm.

Others are made with buckwheat, beer and molasses; Indian slapjack is made from milk, cornmeal, flour and eggs. Simmons's Johnny Cake or hoe cake is baked, and thus more closely resembles cornbread. But there are variants elsewhere that are essentially corn pancakes. The name, it has been claimed, probably erroneously, is a corruption of 'Shawnee Cake' – presumably having been taught to the colonists by Native Americans. In fact another name for these is corn pone, the latter word indeed coming directly from Algonkian. Others speculate that Johnny is a corruption of the word

Hoecakes were probably never cooked on a hoe, though this image suggests a shovel might work.

Cooking buckwheat pancakes on an old-fashioned griddle stovetop in the 1940s.

jonakin, the meaning of which is unknown, or Journey Cake – either because it can be carried on long journeys, which seems unlikely, or because it can be cooked en route, that is if one brings along a hoe. If this technique was really used, it would be quite simple, though advisedly one would want to remove all traces of dirt first. A simple thick batter of fine cornmeal is mixed up with water in the simplest versions, or with milk, eggs and baking powder. Then the flat edge of the hoe is placed on the burning coals. The batter is dropped on and when ready the long handle makes it easy to pass, steaming hot, to hungry campers. A shovel works well too and is a little more useful while camping. No wonder another name for this is ash cake. Another theory insists that hoe cake is a corruption of no cake (meaningless in English) or *nokehick* (meaningful in Narragansett). Perhaps only an enthusiastic food historian could come up with the idea that you could cook on a hoe.

Strangely, however, there was still, even in the nineteenth century, confusion over proper pancake terminology. For example, Lydia Marie Child's *The Frugal Housewife* of 1829 includes a recipe for pancakes in which they are 'boiled

Lurid red pancakes made with beets were a novelty in 19th-century America.

in fat' and are really crisp round fritters. What we know as a pancake, baked on a flat griddle or spider (which comes with its own legs to stand over hot embers) she calls fritters or flat-jacks. Both are made with the same batter: a half pint of milk, 3 spoonfuls of sugar, 1 or 2 eggs, a teaspoon of dissolved pearlash (potassium carbonate, an alkali used as leavening and patented by one Samuel Hopkins in 1790 – actually the very first US patent ever granted). The batter was spiced with cinnamon or cloves, salt and rose water or lemon brandy. In place of eggs, 'lively emptings' can be used (yeast from brewing beer) or, with cornmeal, saleratus is used (an early name for baking soda). Even more interesting is the practice of making pancakes out of 'flip' which is a mug of beer with molasses and a glass of rum, heated with a hot poker until it foams, then thickened with flour (showing a possible connection to flip-jacks or flap-jacks). Remarkably, the flour she refers to is either corn or rye, and even leftover rice can be mixed into the batter.

The willingness to use alternative types of flour seems to have been much greater in the past than today. Sarah Josepha Hale in the *Good Housekeeper* (1841) makes cakes with a quart of buckwheat and a handful of cornmeal leavened with yeast and cold water, nothing more. Made with cornmeal and a little wheat flour, milk and eggs, they are called slapjacks, to be eaten with molasses and butter. But in common with Child, what she calls pancakes are fried in lard, not 'baked' on a griddle.

Eliza Leslie must take the prize for the most original and arresting American variant. In her *Directions for Cookery* (1840) a recipe for the mysteriously titled 'Sweetmeat Pancakes' appears:

Take a large red beet-root that has been boiled tender; cut it up and pound it in a mortar till you have sufficient juice for colouring the pancakes. Then make a batter . . . and stir into it at the last enough of the beet juice to give it a fine pink colour. Or instead of the beet juice, you may use a little cochineal dissolved in a very small quantity of brandy. Fry the pancakes in a pan greased with lard or fresh butter; and as fast as they are done, spread thickly over them raspberry jam or any sort of marmalade. Then roll them up nicely and trim off the ends. Lay them, side by side, on a large dish, and strew powdered sugar over them. Send them to table hot, and eat them with sweetened cream.

'Flannel Cake' is yet another name for pancake; it appears in *What Mrs. Fisher Knows About Southern Cooking* (1881) and consists only of flour and yeast mixed into a batter (the contents of which are not divulged). Soda is also added before baking on a greased griddle. The name presumably derives from the similarity of the final cake to the fabric, or maybe to the shirts of those rugged types who normally eat them.

By the nineteenth century, pancakes were enjoyed by people of every station in society. No less a personage than the chef to Queen Victoria served them. One can almost imagine these being fed in the nursery to the royal brood. This version, however, is meant to edify the lower orders. Charles Elmé Francatelli's *A Plain Cookery Book for the Working Classes* offers a splendidly simple recipe, Pancakes for Shrove Tuesday, worth quoting in full:

Ingredients, twelve ounces of flour, three eggs, one pint of milk, a teaspoon of salt, a little grated nutmeg, and chopped lemon-peel. First, put the flour into a basin, hollow out the centre, add the salt, nut-meg, lemon-peel and a drop of milk, to dissolve them; then break in the eggs, work all together with a spoon, into a smooth soft paste, then add the remainder of the milk, work the whole vigorously until it forms a smooth liquid batter. Next set a fry-ing-pan on the fire, and, as soon as it gets hot, wipe it out clean with a cloth, then run about a teaspoon-ful of lard all over the bottom of the hot frying-pan, pour in half a small teacupful of the batter, place the pan over the fire, and, in about a minute or so, the pancake will have become set sufficiently firm to enable you to turn it over in the frying-pan, in order that it may be baked on the other side also; the pan-cake done on both sides, turn it out on its dish, and sprinkle a little sugar over it: proceed to use up the remaining batter in the same manner.

By the twentieth century, pancakes were everywhere on both sides of the Atlantic – and indeed around the world. The international history of pancakes will be recounted below. For now, we continue the story by focusing on the many roles pancakes have played in the culture of food. By capitalizing on a few basic culinary functions, the pancake has become beloved for a variety of reasons. Pancakes are revered as the quintessential comfort food, a dish suitable for holidays and celebration, a convenient and portable street food, hearty and nutritious working-class provender and, most remarkable of all, they have found their way into fine dining. The following five chapters cover these topics in turn.

There are rich cultural associations with pancakes that change over time and from place to place. For example, in Britain Pancake Day immediately conjures images of raucous celebration and races of pan-wielding runners beckoned by the pancake bell. In the US the broad grinning face of Aunt Jemima, though altered over the decades to disassociate her from the 'mammy' of past generations, still draws forth explicit memories of Sunday morning breakfasts. In the past, the pancake was more readily associated with outdoorsmen, pioneers and loggers, for whom breakfast absolutely had to include a towering stack of buttermilk-laden pancakes swathed in maple syrup and dotted with butter. As a respite from work in the fields, the hoe cake, according to legend, was cooked right on an open fire. Around the globe, different people have decidedly different associations with pancakes, and thus this story is as much about the people who make and consume them as the food itself.

I
Comfort Food

In the western world, pancakes are among the most cherished and quintessential of comfort foods, especially when served for breakfast. This is because they are utterly indulgent and completely predictable. Pancakes taste best consumed in periods of sloth on protracted weekend mornings. They must be savoured without hurry or premeditation, ideally in dressing gown and slippers, at the kitchen table or maybe even in bed, and preferably in excess, just to the brink of nausea. The combination of grease, syrup and flour should create just the right leaden effect on the stomach so as to prevent any further activity for several hours. Park the numb and bloated carcass in a comfortable chair with a newspaper or in front of the TV: the only way to deal with the postprandial stupor. This experience defines comfort.

Such pancakes are supremely comforting when prepared by a loved one. Few foods better epitomize contented domestication. What other food can nestle berries or chocolate chips in a smiley face, or better yet be cooked in a Mickey Mouse mould or poured in the form of the letter B?

Pancakes are normally made from fresh ingredients as they are so simple to prepare but, increasingly, those pressed for time or talent use dry mixes, chilled batters in a carton,

Apparently even dogs like pancakes, as this image of Cary Grant shows.

or even frozen varieties that are popped in the toaster. But for a pancake to be considered homemade, there must be at least a suggestion of actual mixing and frying. Aunt Jemima has recently begun marketing a pancake mix in a plastic jug to which one only adds water, creating an instant batter, removing the mixing bowl step beloved by Bisquick fans, yet still lending the impression of making the pancakes from scratch. That is, it satisfies parents and children that this is something cooked especially for them, of a higher order and status than a box of cold cereal.

Aunt Jemima herself is a perplexing image of comfort, recalling, despite her many makeovers, an antebellum slave mammy, expert in the kitchen and ready at any time to satisfy the hunger pangs of her master and children. Understandably the company has distanced itself from this association, and Jemima now sports a neat coiffure and pearl earrings, sure signs that she is a middle-class black woman, perhaps a working grandmother, serving her own family. In the early twentieth century, however, the association with slavery was very real and Americans seem to have enjoyed buying products they could imagine were fixed by expert black cooks. Blackface minstrels and cakewalks were not yet seen as degrading, at least by most white consumers. Aunt Jemima was first used by Chris L. Rutt and Charles Underwood in St Joseph, Missouri as a vehicle to market their instant pancake mix, which appeared in 1889. Though their Pearl Milling Company went bankrupt, the pancake recipe and Aunt Jemima were bought by the R. T. Davis Milling Company. Davis decided to use a real live woman, one Nancy Green, born into slavery, to be Aunt Jemima in the company's advertisements. She cooked pancakes at the Columbian Exposition at Chicago and drew enormous enthusiastic crowds. She even entertained the throngs at Disneyland with her pancake skills. In 1925 Quaker Oats bought the product and its trademark. Green had died a few years earlier in a car accident but there were replacements for her for many decades.

The history of the advertising image of Aunt Jemima is fascinating in itself, but the irony of selling a mix as something homemade seems to have escaped most people, as it still does. Perhaps the idea was much the same as with instant

Louise Beavers as housekeeper Delilah Johnson in *Imitation of Life* (1934). Loosely modelled on the experience of the woman who portrayed Aunt Jemima, the film explores how the image of black slave women was appropriated to sell pancake mix.

cake mixes: after adding eggs to the dry ingredients, the cook is left with the impression of having actually made something. With pancakes, it is cooking them from a batter that seems to constitute an authentic culinary accomplishment.

What is more perplexing is why the Aunt Jemima icon is still used to sell pancakes. Clearly in the early twentieth century she was a character meant to evoke the idyllic Old South, where the black woman was portrayed as happy to serve as a slave to the white family and to comfort them in any number of ways, including going through the labour of making pancakes so that mother did not have to. The fact that she was plump and jolly also assuaged any guilt over the real horrors of slavery. The *Slave in a Box*, as M. M. Manring has called Aunt Jemima in a book of the same name, does precisely the same thing. She (i.e. the company) does all the work so you can enjoy your leisure and comfort. The box of pancake mix serves the same function as the black slave.

In the twentieth century this product and many others were marketed as 'convenience' foods. Somehow consumers were convinced that the effort of mixing flour, eggs and milk was excessive and that it saved time if you could just pour a dry mix into a bowl. The combination of comfort and convenience reached perhaps the pinnacle of folly in an invention designed to make pancakes automatically at home. On 28 April 1958 *Time* magazine featured an automatic pancake baker designed by the Polarad Electronics Corporation on which 'a hopper at the top holds the batter, releases enough for one pancake at a time to an electronically heated griddle'. The machine then flips it and the 'finished pancakes thus drop onto a platter continuously'. The inventor hoped this would relieve his harried wife from the ongoing effort of plying their voracious hoard of children with pancakes.

We must wonder how such a simple food could retain the association with comfort, despite all these modern conveniences. The answer must be that pancakes are one of the first foods given to children after they are weaned from pap and mush and thus are indelibly associated with childhood and pleasant memories. Not surprisingly they also feature prominently in children's books. Among all the foods mentioned by children's authors, none is more pervasive than pancakes – green eggs and ham notwithstanding. There is a very good reason for this: pancakes are among the simplest, tastiest and most approachable of foods that can be introduced at a young age, hence the deep nostalgia among grown-ups and reveries of happy pancake-filled youth. The pancake is the comfort food that no vegetable or breakfast cereal could ever hope to be. A true comfort food must be

Natalie Wood whips up a pancake breakfast, 1957.

warm and fresh and preferably laboured over by a loved one especially for you. Remember, this is how the witch in Hansel and Gretel is able to lure the children into her house: not only is the roof made of cake and the windows of sugar, but she feeds them milk and pancakes, and only after gaining their trust by cooking for them, does she lock up Hansel and reveal her plan to eat the children.

Knowing full well that children can relate to pancakes, a spate of books includes them – Curious George makes pancakes, *If You Give a Pig a Pancake* is a sequel to the popular mouse and cookie book and there are dozens of lesser-known titles. This is nothing new: 'Little Black Sambo', though now obscure thanks to illustrations and subject matter deemed offensive, was hugely popular over a century ago. Set in India, the story involves a young boy, Sambo, fending off a series of tigers by giving them each an article from his dashing new wardrobe. The tigers end up arguing over which is the most dapper, finally chasing each other around a tree with such vigour that they melt into 'ghi' (clarified butter). The butter is then used by Sambo's mother, Mumbo, to make pancakes. Sambo eats no less than 169. That's contentment for you.

The other locus for pancake comfort, interestingly enough, is outside the home. The passion for pancakes was satisfied in a sheer deluge of so-called pancake houses that began to appear in the 1950s. The Original Pancake House founded in Portland, Oregon in 1953 was among the earliest of these and is still in business today with 90 franchises from coast to coast. But it is minuscule compared to the pancake house giant: the International House of Pancakes, or IHOP, founded in Toluca Lake, a suburb of Los Angeles, in 1958. Numerous national and regional franchises followed, it was traded publicly by 1961 and then went fairly berserk buying up businesses over the next decades, including non-food companies. Today the company appears to have divested these to refocus on pancakes. Today most US cities have one if not several IHOP franchises, with over 900 outlets thriving nationally.

The appeal of most pancake houses, judging from the typical decor, appears to derive from nostalgia for the good old times when people ate simple hearty food in great quantities before they went out to chop firewood or plough the fields. Red checked gingham, at least at the beginning, was the sign of traditional home cooking, despite the fact that most people drove up in cars and allowed strangers to prepare their 'grand-slam' breakfasts. IHOPs all had a very distinctive A-frame with a blue roof and a colonial-looking electrified sign. Many shops intentionally capitalized on the fashion for things colonial in the 1970s, nicely coinciding with the bicentennial celebrations and a surge of patriotism,

A modern incarnation of the International House of Pancakes in Stockton, California.

fostered perhaps in the wake of so much political disaffection during the Vietnam War. In other words, like traditional family values and traditional American style at the time, albeit in a highly kitschy 1970s interpretation, the pancake house became a bastion of comfort with an overtly conservative message. Hippies might be drug-soaked and sexually liberated, but good Americans take their families out to eat pancakes. At least this seemed to be the message that came through in the advertisements of the giant pancake houses.

There have also been loyal patrons of the independent local greasy spoon, where one would at least know the waitress and perhaps even be able to claim a regular spot with a cup of joe and a short stack of flapjacks brought without asking. Smaller independent pancake houses are to be found everywhere in the US. They blend fairly seamlessly into other generic breakfast joints, such as Denny's, which is actually the largest breakfast chain in the US, and has roots in California in the mid-1950s. Diners are typically places where one can get breakfast pancakes any time of day, and they are an older institution than the pancake house. Diners usurped some of the pancake house's function, particularly involving comfort food that can be ordered any time of day, even late at night after a raucous night on the town.

The pancake craze was not merely a US phenomenon. The Netherlands is also riddled with cosy pancakes houses, though there they are more like family restaurants, often not even open in the morning for breakfast. In Britain, the phenomenon is not quite as widespread, though a few pancake houses have been around for a long time.

The association of pancakes with comfort and family values is not a western phenomenon either. In Japan, *dorayaki* have much the same appeal for children and nostalgic adults, though they are more of a sweet treat than a breakfast staple. They are normally two small sweet pancakes with sweet *azuki* bean paste (*anko*) in the middle, though they can also be filled with chestnut or pastry cream. *Dorayaki* have a strange history. Legend says that they were first prepared when the samurai Benkei accidentally left his gong behind at a farmer's house where he was hiding out. The intrepid farmer used it to cook little 'gong cakes' as the word translates literally. But they also have an interesting connection to the Portuguese who arrived in the sixteenth century. *Dorayaki* are made from a kind of cake batter incorporating eggs, flour and sugar in much the same way *kasutera* or sponge cake is made. *Kasutera* is in turn a form of the word *castella* – meaning Castile in Spain – and thus *dorayaki* are related to *pão de Castella* in Portuguese, or *pan di Spagna* in

Dorayaki are usually filled with sweet bean paste, but here they are topped with octopus.

Italian, otherwise known as sponge cake. Today these can be made at home to fill bento boxes for lunch, but little elegant and intensely sweet versions are also mass manufactured and sold in plastic wrappers. They are the favourite food of a famous cartoon character, Doraemon, a robotic cat. Thus the association of *dorayaki* with children is firmly established, just as it is for the pancake in the West, although in form and function perhaps the closest comparison would be with the Twinkie. *Dorayaki* are similar in their cloying sweetness as well as their nostalgic appeal, slightly derisive, as it is with all mass-manufactured junk food. They are enjoyed by adults precisely because grown-ups should not like them; they are regressively infantile, and this in itself is comforting.

An entirely different kind of pancake in Japan is a fairly recent invention called *okonomiyaki*. These are savoury and have just about anything mixed in. In fact, the word means 'as you like it'. The batter is not dairy based but rather a mixture of *dashi* stock (made from dried bonito flakes – a relative of tuna, and *kombu* – giant seaweed), flour and eggs. The Kansai variation originating in the area of Osaka can come with sea-weed, bonito flakes, cabbage, pickles and a sweet brown *okonomi* sauce, or even mayonnaise. Virtually any kind of fish or meat can be included as well. In the end it looks something like a pizza with toppings. In Hiroshima the ingredients are layered instead and served on top of fried noodles.

Special restaurants serve *okonomiyaki* and some let customers cook them on their own little hotplates (*teppan*) at each table, adding whatever they prefer. Others are a kind of lunch counter where patrons are served right from the hot griddle a huge pancake, deftly turned with two spatulas and chopped up before service. They are also served by street vendors and everywhere are a fairly cheap food. They are thus a favourite among students, and shops abound most

Okonomiyaki in Japanese means 'as you like it'.

around university campuses. For many Japanese, *okonomiyaki* are a reminder of that happy time of life, before the onset of professional pressures, family and responsibilities. And because they come in so many varieties, everyone has their own particular favourite. Of course any food that can evoke powerful memories qualifies as a comfort food, but these hugely versatile pancakes hold the same sort of appeal that pizza does for students in the West; they are a food to be shared among close friends. The more ingredients and the stranger the combinations, the greater the sense of ownership, and of course the greater the comfort when one eats just the right kind. A friend, expert in Japanese food, says the mere smell of *okonomiyaki* can bring tears to the eyes of a grown man, nostalgic for his student days.

Comfort can also be derived from something one eats every day and without which a meal seems incomplete. This

comes in the form of rice for most Asians, bread or pasta for Italians. The same holds for the staple of Ethiopia, a behemoth pancake called *injera*. Certainly the prize for the largest and most versatile pancake on earth must go to this dish. It can measure a full 3 feet (90 cm) across and there is good reason for this – it serves as the base onto which an entire meal is heaped in neat little piles. The typical – and not a little opulent – Ethiopian meal normally consists of a *wat*, or stew of chicken or goat, plus various purees of lentils and vegetables, all highly seasoned and extraordinarily spicy. The *injera* can also be served rolled up for each diner to tear bits off to use as a utensil to scoop morsels from the communal platter. When the meal is done the *injera* platter itself is eaten too. *Injera* has a delightfully sour flavour and indescribably delightful spongy texture; one might almost describe it as elastic.

Injera is comforting to Ethiopians precisely because it is the staple, eaten at almost every meal. The best variety is made from teff, a grain that grows here and practically nowhere else. Botanically speaking, teff is *Eragrostis tef*, a

A simple illustration of the domestic division of labour in colonial Abyssinia – women making *injera*, and men consuming them.

delightful name meaning love grass, derived from Eros and *grostis* (grass). It is a minuscule grain that thrives in the dry conditions of the Ethiopian mountains and is extremely labour intensive to cultivate and process. For this reason it is fairly expensive and only wealthier families eat *injera* of pure teff, the lighter coloured varieties being most highly prized, though less flavoursome than darker types. In poorer households the flour is made of a mixture of teff with corn or barley. In Ethiopian restaurants in the US *injera* are often made with regular wheat flour, which is not nearly as interesting. Nor do they last more than a day. In Ethiopia, *injera* are cooked every few days and they remain fresh and pliable.

The careful procedure of making *injera* in Ethiopia.

The huge towel-like *injera* is cooked on a hot flat griddle on one side while covered with a basket lid.

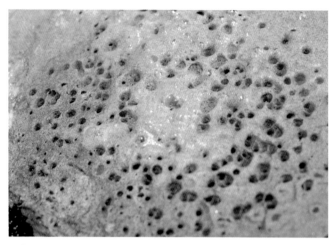

Making *injera* takes a deft hand. They are a staple in Ethiopian cuisine.

The *injera* cooking technique is unique among the pancake tribe. The batter takes a full three days to ferment – with wild yeast in the air. First a thick mash is made from teff flour and water. This is left to sour. The next day water is added to thin it out and this is left another day. On the third day the water on top is poured off and more hot water is added until it is a pourable batter. Then a large flat metal grill without a rim is heated, traditionally over a fire, set low to the ground. Then in some versions cabbage seeds, ground into a fine powder, are sprinkled on the surface. Or oil can be used to moisten the metal. The batter is then poured onto the grill starting from the outside and working inwards in concentric circles. This is covered with a reed-basket top. It is cooked quickly on one side only, the bubbles which appear on the upper surface giving it a lovely sponge- or towel-like texture. Lastly a round woven mat is slid underneath to remove the huge pancake, which is added to a pile.

For Ethiopians, *injera* is the most comforting of foods primarily because there is nothing quite like it anywhere on earth. Only an Ethiopian can distinguish those that are properly made from poor imitations. It is a kind of connoisseurship that comes only from daily experience. Eating authentic *injera* just like mother or grandmother used to make is, for Ethiopians, particularly those in exile, comforting because it conjures up homeland and heritage and confirms identity.

The same is true of the *dosa* (or *dhosa*, *dosai*) of India. Although less well known in the West than chappati, nan, roti and various flat breads of Northern India, the *dosa* is a mainstay of the southern diet. It is structurally similar to the *injera* in that they can both be huge whopping pancakes, wrapped around food or used as little scoops to convey mouthfuls. The *dosa* is also a product naturally soured through wild yeast and made from the local staples, in this case rice and black gram beans (*Vigna mungo*). The procedure is quite simple and yields surprisingly delicate results. First the *urad* dal (which is the shelled bean whose interior is white) is soaked overnight, as is anywhere from two to four times the same quantity of rice, normally in a separate vessel. The next day these are drained and rinsed, then finely ground, traditionally in a huge stone mortar – a very time-consuming process. A blender is a modern option. Water is added to the finely ground paste until it becomes a smooth batter. This is left overnight until bubbly and fragrant. It must not be left too long or it begins to smell really funky. This batter is then used to make a thin crêpe-like disc on a large skillet or *tava*, lightly oiled or with a bit of ghee. In Tamil Nadu the *dosa* is smaller and thicker. It is normally served for breakfast with a *sambhar* (a thin vegetable and lentil stew) or coconut chutney. A masala *dosa* is stuffed with potatoes and fried onions and spices, but the onions can also be put right in the batter. Ground fenugreek seeds are also a common addition to the batter.

While *dosa*s are ordinarily made at home, they also feature prominently in what is called the *udupi*, a restaurant equivalent to the western pancake house, also open early in the morning. They offer only vegetarian food, served on a banana leaf, so orthodox Hindus can eat there without breaking their dietary regulations. The *dosa* also has a place in southern Indian culture as an object of memory and longing since families are often extended and many children grow up with their grandmother or elderly relative preparing *dosa*s every morning. This is how such food traditions are perpetuated through the generations, and why they are such strong reminders of the homeland for expatriates who are faced with unfamiliar and often mass-produced foods. For them, eating *dosa*s is a way to reconnect with their roots in India and, as with the *injera* and many other pancake forms, a way to reassert identity. Evidence of this can be found in

The South Indian *dosa* is rolled up with ingredients inside and served with a dipping sauce.

the long queues of expats to be found waiting for the exquisite *dosa*s served at the southern end of Washington Square Park in Greenwich Village, quite possibly the only cart of its kind in New York City, if not the US. There are also a number of 'Dosa Express' restaurants in New Jersey, mostly serving the burgeoning Indian community there.

2
Celebration

Britons look forward to Shrove Tuesday pancakes, Jewish people the Hanukkah latke, the French their Chandeleur crêpes, and in many countries the pancake in various forms has been hailed as the ideal vehicle for celebration. This chapter will focus on how this came to be: why special holiday pancake versions are found around the world and why they have been set aside as ritually appropriate. It reveals fundamental cultural attitudes toward festivity: as a last buttery fling before Lent, as a grease-laden Christmas treat, or as a respite from grieving after a Russian Orthodox funeral.

One of the most familiar holiday associations with pancakes is Shrove Tuesday, or Pancake Day. The name comes from the verb to shrive, or confess. It falls on the day before Ash Wednesday, the beginning of Lent, when all meat and dairy products have to be foresworn. It is time to confess one's sins in a purification of the soul that matches the physical purification of the body through abstinence. This, of course, means that a wild celebration is in order first, something still known elsewhere as Mardi Gras. How pancakes specifically came to be associated with this day in Britain is a mystery – there are plenty of ways one might dispose of eggs and butter. Perhaps this was the easiest to pull off in a humble kitchen. Recipes for Shrove Tuesday pancakes are in fact far more egg and butter laden than the floury fluffy pancakes familiar to Americans. For example, one recipe includes 4 eggs, a cup/235 ml of whole milk, a tablespoon of melted butter, and 1 tablespoon of sugar to 1 cup/125 g of flour.

Another essential part of the pancake celebration is the ringing of a shriving bell. This was originally meant to call parishioners to confess but, so the story goes, one housewife was still busy cooking pancakes one morning when a particularly zealous vicar rang the bell rather early. Still in her apron she took off, pan in hand, flipping as she went, so as not to spoil the efforts of her labour. This story is celebrated in a traditional pancake race, the oldest of which has been held in Olney, Buckinghamshire since 1445, it is claimed. A more recent revival has made it what it is today – a real competition. Runners must be dress- and apron-clad, wear a bonnet, and must sprint 415 yards (379 metres) while tossing cake before passing the finish line at the church of Saint Peter and Saint Paul. Elsewhere the race has become an occasion for merriment – men dressing in drag and other silliness. There is even a race in Liberal, Kansas, held only since 1950, which in some years beats Olney's record time.

There is another strange pancake custom commonly held in boys' schools which involves the headmaster tossing a pancake over a high bar; on the other side of this the boys scramble for it, ideally catching it whole. At Westminster School in London this is called a 'Pancake Greaze'. The ceremony was also held at Eton and other schools, though how the tossing took this form is a mystery. It dates back several hundred years according to archival records.

Racing and tossing aside, the association of pancakes with this day has been long established. In Shakespeare's *As You Like It* (II.ii.23), the clown, commenting upon the fitness of his answer, says that it is 'As fit as ten groats is for the hand of an attorney, as your French crown for your taffety punk, as Tib's rush for Tom's forefinger, as a pancake for Shrove Tuesday . . .' What he means is that it is as fit as a bribe for a lawyer, hefty payment for a dolled-up whore, a rush ring in a mock wedding, or pancakes, as everyone knows, the essential food of celebration for the days preceding Lent.

In Thomas Dekker's *The Shoemaker's Holiday*, a play full of hilarious food references, Simon Eyre, base-born master of a shoemaking shop, suddenly becomes Lord Mayor of London. Fulfilling a vow made in jest, he mentions that at the sound of the pancake bell, everyone in his shop (whom he derisively refers to as his Mesopotamians) gets the day off: 'I have procured that upon every Shrove Tuesday, at the sound of the pancake bell, my fine dapper Assyrian lads shall clap up their shop windows and away.' And after the plot lines begin to come together towards a happy ending, the bell does sound. Firk the shoemaker then exclaims, 'O brave! O sweet bell! O delicate pancakes! Open the doors, my hearts, and shut up the windows. Keep in the house, let out the pancakes . . .' Eyre's vow was to feed all the apprentices in London should he ever become mayor, and so he does. Hundreds are invited to a new hall to gorge themselves on pancakes and various other enticing dishes for breakfast. How can we explain such ecstatic jubilation over pancakes? It is partly a day off from work, but there is also something socially subversive in it. This is the one day where all men are equal. As Firk says, 'When the pancake bell rings, we are as free as my Lord Mayor.' Free from work, and free to indulge to their hearts' content, something that rarely happens among those who ply the Gentle Craft, which is what they call the shoemaker's trade. And a figure no less than the king

The world's oldest pancake race, in the village of Olney, Buckinghamshire.

joins them on this day, to consecrate the marriage of two main characters, a nobly born man and a common woman, for 'love respects no blood, Cares not for difference of birth or state . . .'. In other words, the pancake bell tolls not only for a day of pigging out, but a socially levelling day when rank and status are briefly dispensed with. The king himself, in the end, partakes of the Shrovetide feast set out for apprentices. The world has been turned upside down for carnival (the Continental name for this same holiday, also known as Mardi Gras) but never truly threatens the social order. The next day everyone goes back to work and, since it is Lent, meat and buttery pancakes are forbidden. But the story itself does hold promise of rising up the social ranks, through marriage, good luck or hard work. It is essentially an optimistic story that some ordinary base-born fellow may get his pancake and eat it too.

Not everyone always took all this merry prankishness in good stride, however. The more puritanical saw it as a remnant of a pagan past never properly purified by the Catholic church, and as potentially subversive in more than a symbolic way. Many sought to ban such celebrations in the 16th and 17th centuries. As the following quote suggests, these celebrations were seen as a kind of illicit magic. The following satirical diatribe levelled at Shrove Tuesday celebrations appears in the 1620 *Jack a Lent, His Beginning and Entertainment* by the satirist John Taylor, best known as the Water Poet. Incidentally, the description of bubbling suet reminds us that the pancake at this time, at least in Taylor's description, is a crisp fritter rather than a floppy cake:

Shrove-Tuesday. At whose entrance in the morning, all the whole kingdom is in quiet, but by that time the clocke strikes eleven, which (by the helpe of a knavish Sexton) is commonly before nine, then there is a Bell rung, call'd the Pancake Bell, the sound whereof makes thousands of people distracted, and forgetfull eyther of manners or humanitie: Then there is a thing cal'd wheaten flowre, which the sulfory Necromanticke Cookes doe mingle with water, Egges, spice, and other tragicall, magicall inchantments, and then they put it by little and little, into a Frying pan of boyling Suet, where it makes a confused dismal hissing, (like the Lernean Snakes in the reeds of Acheron, Stix, or Phlegeton) untill at last, by the skill of the Cookes, it is transform'd into the forme of a Flap-jack, which in our translation is call'd a Pancake, which ominous incantation the ignorant people doe devoure very greedily . . .

This impression is confirmed by a poem in Pasquil's Palinodia of 1634, which also alludes to pancake tossing, if not racing while doing it. On Pancake Day every stomach

> . . . till it can hold no more,
> Is fritter-filled, as well as heart can wish;
> And every man and maide doe take their turne,
> And tosse their pancakes up for feare they burne;
> And all the kitchen doth with laughter sound,
> To see the pancakes fall upon the ground.

Another custom practised on Shrove Tuesday, awful to our modern-day sensibilities, though apparently jolly to those accustomed to bear-baiting and public execution, was called 'threshing the fat hen'. A hen would literally be beaten in turn by youths until dead, and then eaten with the pancakes. There is a marvellous story told in the *Gentlemen's*

Magazine of 1749 of a particular hen that had enough and dared to speak these words:

> Hold thy hand a moment, hard-hearted wretch! if it be but of out of curiosity, to hear one of my feathered species utter articulate sounds. – What art thou, or any of thy comrades, better than I, though bigger and stronger, and at liberty, while I am tied by the leg . . . What have I done to deserve the treatment I have suffered this day, from thee and thy barbarous companions?

The hen continued, with extraordinary elocution, to berate the revellers, particularly upset at her treatment after she had patiently 'furnished thy table with dainties . . . my new laid eggs enriched thy pancakes, puddings and custards.' Alas, the poor bird dropped dead, but her words were recorded for posterity.

Across the Channel, another holiday associated with pancakes is Candlemas, or La Chandeleur. This is celebrated in France on 2 February to commemorate the day Jesus was presented in the Temple by Mary and Joseph. The name for the holiday derives from a chance meeting that day with St Simeon who, after taking one look at the baby, said he would be 'The Light of the World' – hence the lighting of candles on this day. The holiday may even have earlier pagan roots. Children dress up and wear masks, and crêpes are the traditional food eaten. A saying goes, 'Manger des crêpes à la chandeleur, Apporte un an de bonheur.' ('To eat crêpes on Candlemas, Brings a year of happiness.') In the south, the custom is to hold a coin in your left hand while tossing a pancake with the other, which brings wealth in the coming year. Typical of French cuisine, every locality has its own

Tossing a pancake with evident satisfaction and aplomb.

variety of crêpe with its own name. In the north-east are to be found medieval *vautes* which can be filled with apples or cherries. In Argonne to the east they are called *chialades*, and further east in Alsace, *chache-creupé*. In Berry and Limousin they are *sanciauz*, *cruchpeta* in the Basque country and *landimolles* in Picardie. Whatever they are called, they are all the traditional food of celebration for this holiday.

Christianity does not have a monopoly on pancake revels. Hanukkah is a Jewish celebration commemorating the defiant act of the Maccabees and their followers in holding off the siege of their Syrian–Greek (Seleucid) rulers in the

Latkes are a traditional fried potato pancake made for the Jewish festival of lights, Hanukkah.

160s BC. During the siege there was only one day's worth of oil to light the sacred lamps in the Temple, which miraculously lasted eight days. This is why a menorah is lit and also why cakes are fried in oil. Nowadays these are usually potato pancakes or latkes, befitting the eastern European origin of many Jews of Ashkenazic descent. They are not very different from Polish *placki*, made from grated potato and not therefore true pancakes. Before the popularity of the potato in the eighteenth century, the cakes would have been ordinary pancakes or something similar, or perhaps a kind of doughnut. Among Sephardim, originating in Spain, a traditional honey-drenched fritter flavoured with anise is eaten at Hanukkah. This is called *bimuelos*, although the word can also refer to a regular pancake. The term is also used for *bimuelos de massa* – a matzoh meal pancake eaten during Passover, more commonly known as matzoh brie. The unleavened bread or matzoh takes the place of flour which is forbidden during the holiday. Incidentally, the term *bimuelos* is found throughout the Spanish-speaking world. A fritter eaten in Mexico during Christmas, called *buñuelos*, has precisely the same origin.

Throughout Scandinavia there is a jewel of a pancake, deceptively plump and spherical in form, particularly associated with Christmas. Eaten in the evening it is served with *glögg*, a kind of hot mulled wine and fruit juice concoction, but it is also traditional for Christmas morning breakfast both in Scandinavia and among those of Nordic ancestry elsewhere. These are the delightfully named *aebleskiver* (singular *aebleskive*), though one encounters many variations of the name: *abelskiver*, *ebelskiver* and so forth. The name seems to mean apple slice and older recipes do include apple,

The *aebelskiver* is a traditional round pancake popular throughout Scandinavia. It is best made with buckwheat.

though it rarely does any more. They appear to originate with the Danes, though a rather similar pancake called *poffertjes* can be found in the Netherlands. In any case, what makes these unique is the way they are cooked, in a cast-iron pan with little round depressions, known as a munk pan. The batter is poured into the lightly greased craters, where it puffs up. Traditionally it is supposed to be turned over with a knitting needle, though there are also little wooden two-pronged forks especially designed to flip the little pancake balls. The filling, if used, is pressed into the batter before flipping. If unfilled, the pancakes are sprinkled with powdered sugar and served with jam. The batter for these comes in many different forms. In the us Bisquick or Krusteaz mix is sometimes used, and it works. But the more authentic recipes are rather richer and include more eggs and buttermilk. Sometimes the egg whites are beaten and folded in to create a puffier pancake. *Aebleskiver* qualify both as a holiday pancake and a comfort food – they are reserved for a specific holiday morning, use traditional equipment used for no other recipes so the pans tend to become heirlooms, and they are associated with childhood memories, cosy family gatherings and departed relatives. As with all traditional Christmas foods, people form strong attachments to a particular recipe, which is handed down with care to each generation. The holiday celebration in a sense comes to be defined by the presence of *aebleskiver*. Without them the holiday is somehow incomplete. *Aebelskiver* are a concrete connection to the past, incorporated as an expression of ethnic identity.

3
Street Food

One of the distinguishing features of most types of pancake is their eminent portability. When engineered to be rolled around a filling or to encase finely chopped ingredients, they are cheap, filling and make the perfect street food. Vendors with a limited amount of fuel, at first probably a frying pan and a small fire of scrap wood, could turn out pancakes to order for hungry passers-by. Since they cook in a few minutes and are best eaten hot, customers receive their food quickly and move on while munching their snack *à pied*. This is probably why variations on pancakes made with a staggering range of ingredients can be found around the world, and why all share a basic affinity. Street pancakes are normally fatter and sturdier than floppier breakfast pancakes, especially if the filling is inside, though not if the customer is supplied with a disposable plate. Pancakes such as the French crêpe, on the other hand, are larger and rolled or folded around the fillings, but are no less portable. Crêpe stands with their specially designed flat rimless griddles are a common sight throughout France, as are other portable pancakes throughout the world.

Socca is a unique form of pancake made with chickpea flour, variations of which are found all along the southern

Pancakes sold on the streets in war-torn Paris.

Mediterranean coast. *Farinata* is a close relative from Genoa, the street version being rather thick and crunchy, and commonly eaten by breaking little pieces off with the fingers. *Socca* are extremely simple to make. The batter is made from water, olive oil and chickpea flour, seasoned with salt and a lot of pepper and poured into a tray. It is baked in an extremely hot wood-fired oven. *Socca* can also be made like regular crêpes. In Nice they are sold in the market by the Cours Saleya and in shops in the Old City, and must be eaten while strolling.

In South and Central America there is an entire family of corn-based pancakes ideally suited for carrying away from street stands, eaten any time of day, including late night after dancing. While we have already excluded tortillas and other flat breads made from dough or masa, there are many others which come so close to pancakes, being made from batter, that they must be discussed. *Cachapas*, found in Venezuela, are made from ground fresh corn traditionally pounded, today blended into a batter and fried on a griddle. They are normally covered with *queso blanco*, a white cheese, and folded over. The beauty of them is their simplicity and subtle sweetness and the fact that they can be bought on the street, and eaten while walking. (The word *cachapa* is also slang for lovemaking between two women, the reason for which will have to be left to the reader's imagination.)

Making *cachapas* with the type of corn on the cob found in the US and Europe is a little difficult, and one must add some cornmeal and milk to make a proper batter that will adhere. In South America the corn used is starchier and will hold on its own. Any white cheese will work, including mozzarella, but anything that overwhelms the simple taste of the fresh corn should be avoided.

Similar to the *cachapa* and also hailing from Venezuela are the ubiquitous fluffy little discs called *arepas*. These are made of a pre-cooked ground corn flour which is moulded

Cachapas are savoury pancakes from Venezuela.

by hand and grilled into a little cake. This is then split and filled with cheese, meat or virtually anything. *La reina pepiada* is the most traditional, made with ground meat, avocado and cheese, but others contain pork, chicken or can even be sweet with jam. Other varieties more closely approximate pancakes, such as the *arepa* of Colombia, flatter and thinner, and that of Costa Rica, poured from a batter and indisputably a pancake. Mexican *gorditas* and El Salvadorean *pupusas* can also be considered corn pancake cousins. All can be bought in shops or stands (*areperas, pupuserias*) that effectively compete with fast-food stands selling hamburgers, hot dogs and the like. Apart from the variety of condiments now added they are essentially the same as those made hundreds of years ago by Native Americans, before they had any contact with Europeans.

Moving across the Atlantic we come to Morocco, which boasts a very fine street-food pancake called *beghrir*. These are unique, being made with semolina flour and raised with yeast. They are also enriched with milk, eggs and honey. Being cooked only on one side, *beghrir* have a spongy surface of big gaping holes not unlike *injera*, although the diameter of the pancakes is much smaller. In French they are sometimes called *crêpes mille trous* – or crêpes with a thousand holes. When sold on the street they are usually arranged overlapping in a circular decorative mound and are doused with honey and butter which seeps into the holes. As well as being a street food they are also one of the foods eaten during Ramadan – after sundown. Ramadan is the Muslim fast during which nothing can be eaten until the evening, when the fast is broken with the *f'tour*, an evening feast.

Funkaso is a traditional pancake of West Africa, made simply from millet flour and water. It is similar to the Ethiopian *injera*, but smaller and easier to make. It is fer-

Beghrir, from Northern Africa, have holes on top from being cooked on one side.

mented for several hours to give it a lighter texture. It is usually considered breakfast food among the Hausa, but for those on the move, it can be eaten as a snack on the street.

It is perhaps in Asia that the portable pancake achieves its full efflorescence. On the streets in Thailand one can buy little elegant rice and tapioca starch pancakes called *pak moh*. Taxonomically they are something like a cross between a pancake and a dumpling. *Pak moh* are unlike any other type of pancake in that they are essentially steamed. A little pot steamer covered with a piece of cloth is set on the hot surface. The batter is poured over the cloth and the whole is covered with a conical lid. After the pancake is steamed, fillings are added and the pancake folded over and served. The fillings include coconut, pork, shrimp, bean sprouts and various vegetables. As for most street foods, these are an irresistible combination of flavours and textures: partly soft, partly crunchy, sour with sweet, savoury and spicy. If you stop to consider the most successful of street foods, what they have in common is that they are not only easily carried, but often form a kind of analogue of a complete meal with many different flavours combined. Even a hamburger with its savoury meat, crunchy lettuce, sweet ketchup and sour pickle is basically a small but complete meal. Such combinations are of course common in Thai food, but the *pak moh* in particular meet all the requirements of an ideal street food.

At home *pak moh* can be made easily, with a little practice, by fitting a thin cotton cloth or tea towel over a small pot of steaming water. It can be tied down with string or a sturdy rubber band. Lightly oiling the cloth helps when removing the pancake later. The batter is made of 2 parts rice flour and 1 part tapioca starch (both available in South East Asian groceries), water and salt. It is spread on the cloth thinly and a cover placed over. This must not touch the pancake, so you really need a dome-shaped lid or an inverted bowl. After two or three minutes, put some filling on the pancake, deftly fold over and carefully remove. The filling can be anything to hand, pre-cooked and seasoned with coriander, coconut, fish sauce and so forth.

A cousin of *pak moh* can be found in Indonesia. *Dadar gulung* is made by wrapping cooked sweetened coconut or sometimes sweet beans, jackfruit or nuts around a bright green rice flour pancake coloured with pandan leaf. *Dadar* basically means omelette and *gulung* to roll. It is eaten as a snack food, bought from vendors on the street, or as dessert

Egghoppers, a Sri Lankan dish consisting of a thin crêpe with a fried egg on top.

at sit-down meals. It is not steamed, but fried on a griddle like other pancakes, although the fillings are similar to those found in *pak moh*.

The same is true of the Vietnamese and Cambodian *bánh xèo*. These are turmeric-laden, bright orange, paper-thin pancakes made of rice flour and coconut milk, also sold on the streets as a snack. It is pronounced *bun-shee-ow*, some say onomatopoetically imitating the sound of the batter as it hits the hot pan. They contain basically the same ingredients as spring rolls: crunchy cabbage, coriander, bean sprouts, mushrooms, shrimp and pork. They are folded in half and eaten dipped in a mixture of fish sauce, garlic, hot chillies and lime juice.

All these Asian pancake varieties fit the bill as street food. All come in different colours, use different basic starches and cooking techniques and are essentially unrelated to western pancakes.

In Malaysia and Singapore one encounters *murtabak*. Although similar to other South East Asian pancakes, they are actually made from a thick, rolled-out dough, and so are not really pancakes at all.

However, we might include in this group the Korean *bin-ja tuk*, a pancake made from mung beans ground and thinned into a batter which is then poured onto a griddle. On top slices of pork and *kim-chi* (fermented spicy cabbage) are spread and then the whole flipped over. The most popular of Korean varieties is entirely different. It is called *Hodduk* or *Ho-dduk*, and is bought on the street, usually in winter. In contrast to previous examples, it is sweet, filled with a brown sugar paste or cinnamon and honey with sesame seeds or walnuts inside. *Dduk* is the generic term for the traditional Korean cake, of which there are hundreds of varieties, eaten for various occasions.

Banh Xeo are said to get their name from the sizzling sound made in the pan.

On a side note, it is interesting that there is virtually no street-food pancake in the English-speaking world. This may be the result of our addiction to runny syrupy fillings, or the strong association with breakfast or with particular events. But at this point we should mention the ice-cream cone, essentially a crispy medieval pancake, rolled into a cone and filled – a very distant descendant of the pancake.

4
Working-class Food

There is no need to elaborate on pancakes as filling and nutritious food, perfectly suited for mining camps, lumberjacks and the urban proletariat. Their low cost means they can be eaten in vast quantities and for all cultures that subsist on starchy grains, the pancake is a prime form of easily made nourishment. From hash-slinging diners to tiny makeshift kitchens in the furthest corners of the globe turning out *akara* or *dosa*s, pancakes have provided invaluable sustenance for the working classes.

The association of pancakes as an ideal food for the working classes is particularly apparent after the advent of the proletarian class proper in the nineteenth century – those with limited funds and even more limited cooking facilities. But earlier, rural labourers were already enamoured of pancakes, partly because the necessary ingredients were normally at hand on a country farm. William Ellis in the *Country Housewife's Family Companion* (1750) offers an entire chapter on pancakes and 'How commodiously Pancakes answer the Farmers, the Yeomens, and Gentlemens Interest'. He continues, 'Pancakes are one of the cheapest and more serviceable dishes of a farmer's family in particular; because all the ingredients of the common ones are of his own

Domestic genre painting of pancake cooking.

produce, are ready at hand upon all occasions, saves firing, are soon cook'd are conveniently portable, and supply both meat and bread . . .' What he means is that the milk and eggs in most pancakes take the place of meat for poorer families, but even wealthier farmers (yeomen) and gents can use them as a matter of economy. On the other hand, there is also a pancake made with slices of pickled pork right in the batter, as well as a bacon pancake which 'serves well to fill our plowmens and others bellies instead of intire flesh'. These sound rather like Swedish *flaeskpannkaka* or flesh-pancakes, another food associated with farmers. Ellis continues at length about the ordinary cheap pancake of Hertfordshire, a simple concoction of wheat flour, milk, egg and ginger batter, fried in lard and best flipped, and eaten hot so it doesn't rise in the stomach. Should milk be lacking, it can also be made with beer – not as tasty as with milk 'but where the bellyful is mostly consulted, it will do well enough'.

Ellis gives us a glimpse of the eating habits of ordinary working farmers and the importance of pancakes in their diet. Poor people are addressed – day-labouring men's wives make their pancakes from flour and water, and somehow powdered ginger too which, from his comments, appears to have been cheaper than either sugar or milk. His recipe for 'rich People' is naturally a much richer pancake laden with butter and cream, much like those found in contemporary eighteenth-century English cookbooks.

Pancakes have also been a traditional staple among working Americans, especially those engaged in hard work in the hinterlands, such as loggers and miners. The simplicity and speed of cooking pancakes ideally recommends them to such working conditions. The flour is easily transportable and a quick hot fire is enough to fry them up in a

A woman lost in reverie as she flips pancakes for breakfast, Maine, 1942.

Pancakes were a reminder of home for US soldiers in World War II.

cast-iron pan. The same holds true for field workers and their midday meal, especially if they are working a good distance from home.

There are significant regional variations in pancakes among working types, not only in the ingredients, but also in the preferred topping. In the South the traditional syrup on pancakes is made of sweet sorghum, which was introduced from Africa in the nineteenth century. In the North, maple syrup prevails. There is a tradition that the tapping of maple was learned from Native Americans. This may be true, but the process of boiling it down into syrup was probably invented by the colonists, as a substitute for the more familiar golden syrup made from sugar, or treacle. Today both these have been completely supplanted by maple, though much of this is artificially flavoured with fenugreek or synthetic flavourings and corn syrup.

One of the most cherished characters in American folklore is the lumberjack, clad in red plaid flannel with boots and braces (US: suspenders), and notorious for his Bunyanesque appetite. How lumberjacks came to be associated with stacks of flapjacks, a sort of pancake, over all other foods is unknown, but presumably this was one of the easy-to-make and filling foods that could be prepared in great quantities in short order by cooks in the lumber camps. It may also have resulted from breakfast being an especially filling meal, fuelling the body for the day's hard labour to follow. When one thinks of what lumberjacks eat, pancakes are naturally included. And of course Paul Bunyan, the greatest of lumberjacks, employed a cook named 'Sour Dough Sam' who cooked the flapjacks on a griddle so big that it had to be greased by men with bacon strapped to their feet, who would skate across the metal surface. As the cook's name suggests, flapjacks were often made with a sourdough starter, that is, a bubbly wild yeast 'mother' kept alive and continually replenished with fresh flour and water after each batch. To prepare batter for cooking, some of the starter is mixed with fresh flour and water to form a sponge, in which the yeast grows, usually overnight. The next day this is cooked for breakfast. Like lumberjacks, trappers and mountain men would also have come to depend on their sourdough starter, not usually for bread as might be supposed given current sourdough usage, but principally for those without ovens or those in the hinterland, including farmers on the frontier. The advantage of using wild yeast is that it can be stored in a loosely fitted crock and will remain potent indefinitely if well maintained.

The word flapjack is itself interesting and of much earlier origin than the Old West. Even Shakespeare uses it in *Pericles* when a fisherman says, 'we'll have flesh for holidays, fish for/fasting-days, and moreo'er puddings and flap-jacks.'

The term quite likely derives from the word flap – to turn over, or, as we say today, to flop or flip. As we have seen, it was one of the terms used in early America, and perhaps the common 'jack' ending endeared it especially to lumberjacks. 'Jack' normally meant an ordinary bloke, a rough and merry working-class fellow. Another term used in the late eighteenth century and thereafter was flannel cake, again perhaps from association with the lumberjack's attire.

Miners have been associated with pancakes in the popular imagination – and in real life, it seems. For example, Old Pancake was the nickname for Henry Comstock, after whom the fabulously rich silver mines around Virginia City, Nevada, are named. Comstock was in fact a bit of a loudmouth and scoundrel: he swindled his way into sharing the claim for the discovery of these deposits, later sold it, and met an ignominious end when he committed suicide in Montana. In any case, he is said to have got his nickname from the principle article of his diet, namely pancakes. In the Yukon gold rush of the 1890s, miners were often called 'sourdoughs' and they are said to have slept with their starter to prevent it from freezing.

Cowboys too have definite pancake affinities, as demonstrated in the short story 'The Pimienta Pancakes' by the master of this genre, O. Henry. In it a smooth-talking, pistol-wielding cowpuncher is outmanoeuvred in the affections of a young lady by a dapper sheep rancher, who insists that his interests are purely gastronomic: he seeks the perfect pancake, which the young lady guards as a family secret. The cowboy is sent to wrest the recipe, and the sheep rancher promises to stay away. Little does the cowboy know, his rival has forewarned the lady and her uncle that if the topic of pancakes comes up, the cowpoke is delirious from a previous frying pan assault and must be calmed down. In the end the ruse works: the sheep rancher marries the girl and the cowboy is jibed for ever after about the pancake episode.

The working-class associations with pancakes can be found throughout the world. For example, the most unique of French crêpes is of Gaelic origin – the Breton galette, a long-time staple of the impoverished farmer of north-west France. In the Breton language it is called *krampouz*, a word related to the Welsh *crempog*, which generally means a little pancake, which indicates a very ancient common provenance. In Brittany it is made with flour milled from buckwheat (*Fagopyrum esculentum*, actually not a grain at all but a distant relative of rhubarb). Buckwheat became the staple in this part of France because wheat is harder to grow in the poor wet soils. It was probably introduced in the fifteenth century by the Dutch, despite the name *sarrasin* which suggests that it was brought by the Saracens or Moors. Since rural Brittany throughout the early modern period was relatively impoverished, buckwheat in gruel and galettes became one of the primary sources of calories for the working classes.

Unlike an ordinary crêpe, the galette is somewhat salty, cooked only on one side and filled with savoury ingredients such as Gruyère, ham and eggs (complète), or creamed mushrooms and chicken. There is even a galette with sardines. The galette can be wrapped around a simple sausage, making it portable and common at festivals. The savoury types are usually eaten seated in a little galette shop and, interestingly, their edges are often folded into a square rather than being rolled. Ideally they should be served with a ceramic mug of cold cider. Traditionally they were also dipped into *lait ribot* (buttermilk). Long ago they would have been made on a round iron griddle with three legs set over the fire – a *pillig* in Breton, or *galéatoire*. Today there are electric versions. A little implement, basically a stick with a short cross bar on the end, called a

Paper-thin crêpes are made by raking the batter across the griddle with a *rozelle*.

rozelle, or *rouable*, is then used to spread the batter out as thinly as possible. It is a very neat trick: the implement is swirled in a circular motion across the surface of the still liquid batter, resulting in a paper-thin buckwheat crêpe.

A descendant of the buckwheat galette, eaten in French-speaking Acadie in Canada and Maine, is the *ploye* or *plogue*. The name seems to suggest some connection to the verb *plier*, meaning to fold over, though this may be a false etymology. *Ployes* can be eaten sweetened with syrup, but traditionally are spread with a thick pork spread called *cretons*, something like rillettes, still eaten in France in rural locales. Interestingly, the flour here is called *bockouite* which sounds like a Frenchified English or Dutch term, rather than *sarrasin*, as it is called in France. They are revered today as a reminder of the hard-working French settlers' life of colonial days.

Pancakes are commonly eaten by the urban proletariat, no doubt because of cheap ingredients and limited cooking

Cooking galettes on a street-stall.

facilities. Alexis Soyer's nineteenth-century *Shilling Cookery for the People* offers an appropriate recipe. Although Soyer would have used four eggs when making the dish for his wealthy patrons, perhaps with apples or sultanas and a bit of ginger, he also mentions a very simple version. 'Two eggs only may be used, but in this case use a little more flour and milk.' In the modest household these pancakes would be adorned with nothing more than a sprinkle of sugar and a few drops of lemon.

Lest we should conclude that pancakes are only beloved by those of modest means, we turn finally to the most elaborate pancake creations, those adopted by restaurateurs and gourmands – the haute cuisine pancakes.

1397 (N° 8). Comment on fait une Crêpe bretonne — On la plie
Les Industries Bretonnes

A woman displays the correct procedure for making crêpes in turn of the century France.

5
Fine Dining

Ironically, despite their simplicity and cheap ingredients, pancakes have taken their place among the most elegant and refined of foods. How blini, crêpes or great stacks of jam-laden pancakes through eastern Europe have been featured in fine restaurants is a story both fascinating and remarkable. The elevation of such a humble food is mostly thanks to the pancake's eminent versatility. With the right accompaniments, a dash of expensive liqueur or dollop of caviar, the sweet or savoury pancake is indeed fit for the grandest of repasts.

The most fashionable of all sophisticated pancakes are without doubt Russian blini. The large folded version as well as the tiny caviar and sour cream-topped hors-d'oeuvre really gained international attention among culinary professionals in France. The late nineteenth-century fashion for all things Russian brought caviar and the like, but even before then blini were found in cookbooks, though sometimes associated with Poland. The great Antonin Carême in *L'Art de La Cuisine Française* (1833) has an appropriately grand and exotic recipe for 'blignis' made with milk, rice flour (from crushed and sieved Carolina rice), leavening and eggs. With an extraordinarily precise procedure involving two pans and a

In Russia blini are a traditional New Year's food served with champagne or vodka.

pot of clarified butter, he confects a light, evanescent hors-d'oeuvre. They can also be made of wheat flour or buckwheat – the latter of which was originally used.

Blini certainly did not start out as haute cuisine. The first form of the word in Old Slavic was *mlin*, coming from the word to mill, distinguishing them from unmilled grains eaten as porridge. The associations with blini (blin in the singular) are ancient and extremely rich in Russia. Normally they are eaten during Shrovetide, as are pancakes in other countries. Even pre-Christianity, the ancient Slavs celebrated a rite of spring which featured bright round blini – supposedly intended to represent the return of the sun. Today this is *Maslenitsa*, exactly the same as Shrove Tuesday, and Russian pancake week (actually 'butter week') is much like the British

Pancake Day, though reckoned using a different calendar. As with Mardi Gras, there were traditionally masks and revelry before the onset of Lent, when a great bedecked personification of Lady Maslenitsa was stripped of her finery and burned along with any remaining blini, in a great bonfire, the ashes of which served as a propitiatory sacrifice to the earth. Since the fall of the Soviet Union celebrations like this have been revived in some quarters after a hiatus of many decades.

Blini are also commonly served after funerals in Russia. In Dostoevsky's last novel, *The Brothers Karamazov*, at little Ilusha's funeral: 'It's all so strange, Karamazov, such sorrow and then pancakes after it, it all seems so unnatural in our religion.' The logic of this, as in many cultures, is to celebrate the departed, to distract the mourners with something comforting. Some claim it is also to usher in renewal and rebirth in eternal life, symbolized by the eggs in pancakes.

Blini should be distinguished from *blinchiki*, which do not include yeast and are rolled around fillings. This word is also the origin of the word blintz, which is disqualified from being a pancake since it is fried until crisp. As for cooking proper blini, this is done in a set of little 6-inch pans specially designed for the purpose. The first, of course, never comes out properly, as is recounted in a proverb where the first is always fed to the dog.

Blini can be used as a symbol of hospitality, offered to guests. There is a wonderful anecdote told by an English woman travelling through the Tartar steppes of eastern Russia in the mid-nineteenth century. Lucy Atkinson, in *Recollections of Tartar Steppes* (1863), tells how she arrived in Ekaterinburg just in time for the carnival. 'In each house you enter during this week, and at whatever time of day it may be, you are expected to partake of a blini, a kind of pancake, only much lighter, served with clarified butter and caviar, which latter no one appears to understand that I cannot eat it, especially after living in Russia such a number of years.' Refusal is taken as ingratitude and lack of respect for a traditional expression of welcome and good tidings. Only the best is reserved for guests on such special occasions. It is perhaps fitting that today, miniature blini are most often served on New Year's Eve in the West as one of the most expensive and elegant of foods.

Palacsinta is another of the great pancake creations. Its origins are Hungarian, though it is equally popular elsewhere in eastern Europe. It began as a simple pancake, normally served with jam inside and folded into quarters, but achieved apotheosis at the great court of the Austro–Hungarian Empire. It should only be eaten with Johann Strauss, or better yet Liszt, playing in the background and people waltzing around the table. *Palatschinken* is the name used in Austria, and both names derive from the Latin placenta, meaning cake, perhaps by way of the Romanian term for cake: *plàcintà*, though today this refers to a flaky kind of pastry made from a phyllo or strudel-like dough.

There are savoury versions stuffed with chopped veal (*hortobágyi*) or ham (*sonkas*), rolled and baked with a paprika-spiked sour cream sauce. But the ultimate version is a towering stack of 'slipped' cakes (*csúsztatott* – presumably because each cake is slipped from the pan on top of the next one) served plain or laced with nuts and chocolate sauce, perhaps bananas, then cut in wedges like a cake. There are literally hundreds of variations.

One might not expect to find haute cuisine pancake devotees in South America, but indeed the classic form of pancake and the name, if slightly altered, thrive there. *Panqueque de dulce de leche*, literally 'pancake with sweet milk', is swathed in a magnificently rich reduction of milk and

Palacsinta were served in the great courts of the Austro–Hungarian Empire.

sugar. These Argentine pancakes fully deserve to be included among the most elegant of all varieties. We might also include a lesser-known though no less magnificent version of the pancake. Also with humble origins, though today found in expensive inns through the US South, these are sweet potato pancakes, made from cooked and mashed sweet potatoes (*Ipomoea batatas*, not to be confused with true yams), mixed with flour, eggs and milk into a batter and then fried. Topped with maple syrup and pecans, the result is one of the most divine flavour combinations imaginable.

But of all haute cuisine pancake creations, none is more famous than Crêpes Suzette. The legend of their creation goes back to 1895 (or 1896 in some accounts) where they were said to be invented by accident by one Henri Charpentier at the Café de Paris in Monte Carlo. As a fourteen-year-old apprentice making crêpes to be served to the Prince of Wales, the future Edward VII, Charpentier accidentally let the cordials in the sauce catch fire. Finding the result sublime, he served it to the regal party. Crêpes Princesse was put forward as a name, but the Prince himself suggested Crêpes Suzette in honour of a woman present in the party (perhaps a mistress), and the name stuck. Charpentier was later sent a ring, a panama hat and a cane for his act of homage and masterful culinary triumph.

In some versions of the story Suzette was merely the daughter of one of the gentlemen present. In others she was an actress named Suzette (or Suzanne) Reichenburg, who was plied with pancakes by a Monsieur Joseph of the Marivaux Restaurant, to use on stage at the Comedie Française in her role as a serving girl. Lastly a chef, Jean Rédoux, is said to have created them for Princess Suzette Carignan to aid her in her bid for the affections of King Louis XV. In some accounts it's Louis XIV, and Rédoux is also said to have published a cookbook, *Parfait Confiturieur* (*sic*) in 1667. In fact, the great chef François Pierre de La Varenne was the author of the book *Le Parfait Confiturier* which appeared in 1667, published by Jean Ribou. The book contains nothing that resembles a crêpe – it is about candying. Even in La Varenne's book on pastry-making, *Le Patissier François*, there is nothing like a pancake, prompting the English translator, 'Mr. Marnettè', to add a section on 'Pan Cake, according to the Flemish and Holland Fashion and the which as it seems was omitted in this treatise'. In other words, the classic founding text of French cuisine is silent on the topic of crêpes.

But the author whose work represents the pinnacle of this tradition is not silent. August Escoffier penned the first printed reference to Crêpes Suzettes. He called them Suzette pancakes, as if the idea were English, though he did work at

Crêpes Suzette are the classic French dessert pancake.

the Ritz in London. Here the pancakes are flavoured with curaçao, tangerine juice and brandied butter. Then a sauce is made of sugar, butter and orange juice. The flaming procedure uses a cocktail of Cointreau or curaçao with rum or Benedictine, then some brandy or Grand Marnier before the final incendiary fillip. Today Crêpes Suzette are usually made of regular thin crêpes in a sauce of orange juice, sugar and orange zest, flamed with Grand Marnier.

Afterword

As we have seen, pancakes are not only ubiquitous through-out the world, but they are players of countless roles – as leading stars on the dessert buffet, as homey ballast fed to hungry children and hard-working men, as street food in the far-flung corners of the earth. They are elegant and simple, rustic and sophisticated, familiar and exotic. Is there any food that serves so many people in so many ways? And yet, they are all essentially the same product, all mere batter cooked in a pan.

To end, I offer a little pancake rhyme by the poet Christina G. Rossetti (1830–1894). She was the sister of Dante Gabriel Rossetti and is pictured in his painting *The Girlhood of Mary Virgin*. I entreat you, if this essay has aroused grumblings of the belly, to take her advice this very minute.

> Mix a pancake,
> Stir a pancake,
> Pop it in the pan;
> Fry the pancake;
> Toss the pancake,
> Catch it if you can.

Pancake preparation.

Recipes

Kentucky Derby Pancakes

Ingredients
2 cups / 250 g flour
½ teaspoon baking powder
1 egg
½ shot of bourbon
1 capful vanilla essence
milk (enough to make a fairly stiff batter)
1 cup / 110 g pecan nuts
1 cup / 200 g sugar
pinch each of cinnamon, nutmeg and salt
1 small tart apple
a pat of butter for frying
sorghum syrup to top

Begin by mixing the flour, baking powder, egg, bourbon, vanilla essence and milk. Next take the pecans and put them in a pan with the sugar, cinnamon, nutmeg and salt. Cook slowly over a low heat until the sugar melts and begins to stick to the nuts. Stir until they are completely coated, being careful not to burn them, and remove to a dish to cool. Peel and grate the apple. Fry in butter until golden brown. Let cool for a few minutes and add to the batter. Fry the pancakes in butter. Top with the candied nuts and a drizzle of sorghum syrup.

Okonomiyaki (as I like it)

Ingredients
1 ½–2 cups / 200–250 g *okonomiyaki* flour mix (available from
any Japanese grocery)
water
napa cabbage, finely shredded
bean sprouts
snow peas
any leftover vegetables
vegetable oil for frying
bonito shavings
dried seaweed flakes
okonomiyaki sauce (available from any Japanese grocery)
Japanese mayonnaise

Make a batter with the *okonomiyaki* mix (regular wheat flour will not work since it does not contain Japanese yam flour or dashi seasonings) and water. Add all the vegetables and fry in one huge honking pancake. It will take two spatulas to turn it over. When cooked, which will take some time, put it on a plate and sprinkle with the bonito shavings and dried seaweed flakes. I prefer furikake with sesame seeds and dried bits of egg, but any kind will work. Then garnish garishly with *okonomiyaki* sauce (a sort of brown sweet barbecue sauce) and the mayonnaise – which must be squeezed from an obscene little Kewpie doll-shaped bottle. Tuck in with friends.

Okonomi-tonnato

This is a variation on *okonomiyaki*, which I have actually eaten and enjoyed.

Ingredients
2 cups / 250 g *okonomiyaki* flour
water
1 small can tuna in oil, drained

2 tablespoons capers
½ a red pepper, finely diced
pinch of smoked Spanish paprika (Pimentón de la Vera)
vegetable oil or butter for frying

Mix the *okonomiyaki* flour with enough water to make a batter.
Add directly to this the tuna, capers, red pepper and paprika. Fry
these ingredients by the spoonful and serve as an appetizer with
a dry sherry.

Chilli-corn Pancakes

Ingredients
1 ½ cups / 185 g stoneground white cornmeal
2 tablespoons melted butter
1 tablespoon baking powder
milk (enough to make a very firm batter)
1 ancho chilli (canned and drained, or dried and
soaked), finely chopped
¼ cup / 45 g cooked black beans

For the Guacamole
1 ripe tomato
1 avocado
½ small onion, finely diced
juice of 1 lime
pinch of salt

Add to the stoneground white cornmeal the melted butter, baking
powder, milk, ancho chilli and black beans. Mix ingredients together to form a batter. Cook the batter as small pancakes or in a
greased mould for corn sticks, madeleines or miniature muffins at
350°F (180°C) for 10 minutes or until lightly browned. Serve with
guacamole made with the tomato, avocado, onion and lime juice,
all pounded together in a mortar with a good pinch of salt to taste.
Serve with a shot of añejo tequila.

Berry Explosion Pancake

Ingredients
2 cups / 240 g wholewheat flour
1 egg
1 teaspoon baking soda
shot of framboise eau de vie
1 teaspoon demerara sugar
milk (enough to make a smooth loose batter)
butter for frying
any combination of blueberries, blackberries,
raspberries, currants etc.

Begin by making a smooth, loose batter by mixing together the wholewheat flour, egg, baking soda, framboise eau de vie, demerara sugar. Fry the pancakes in the butter and, before turning, drop the berries into the cooking batter. Push them slightly under the surface of the batter, covering with a little extra batter if necessary. Flip and continue cooking. The berries should stay whole but will explode and ooze when the pancake is eaten. These need only a dusting of powdered sugar to serve.

Matzoh Brie (Pronounced Br-eye)

Ingredients
2 pieces of matzoh, broken up into small pieces
3 eggs
salt
sugar to taste
cinnamon to taste
butter for frying

Soak the matzoh in water for about 2 minutes. Then squeeze out the water and add the eggs, salt to taste, sugar and cinnamon. Fry by the ladleful in butter, being sure to flatten the mixture so they are in fact pancakes. Turn over when browned. Serve sprinkled with more sugar and cinnamon. Heretics such as myself will add such unorthodox ingredients as turkey, capers, mustard and cheese and then go so far as to scramble them in the pan – de-pancaking them as an act of defiance. These, for me at least, are cause to celebrate.

Margaret (Carlstein) Hunter's Buttermilk Ebelskivers

Ingredients
3 eggs
2 tablespoons sugar
grated rind of ½ lemon
2 ½ cups/590 ml buttermilk
1 teaspoon baking soda
1 teaspoon baking powder
½ teaspoon salt
1 ½ cups/190 g flour
butter
peeled, sliced apple

Beat eggs well, add sugar, lemon rind and buttermilk. Sift baking soda, baking powder, salt together with flour. Stir into buttermilk. Mix until moistened but do not beat. Heat a teaspoon of butter in each depression of the ebelskiver pan. When sizzling, fill hole half full of batter. When edges of batter begin to brown and the ball becomes cooked, put a small slice of apple on top and then turn the ball with a fork or chopstick to cook the other side.

(These can also be made with buckwheat flour, which yields extraordinary results.)

La Socca (adapted from a Niçoise postcard)

Ingredients
1 pint /470 ml water
2 tablespoons olive oil
2 cups /185 g chickpea flour
salt and pepper

Put water and olive oil into a bowl, add the chickpea flour and whisk well to avoid lumps forming. Season with salt and pepper and strain through a sieve before spreading a thin layer (¼-inch thick) on a greased baking tray. Bake on a pre-heated barbecue grill on high heat with the lid closed. Or use a wood-fired oven. Season with freshly ground black pepper and serve immediately, cut up and eaten with the fingers.

Cachapas (adapted for us and British kitchens)

Ingredients
2 cups /275 g cornmeal
1 cup /155 g fresh corn cut from the cob
1 green and 1 red pepper, finely diced
1 jalapeño, seeded and chopped
pinch of baking soda
salt
a little milk for moistening
butter for frying
1 slice of cheese, either queso blanco,
mild white cheese or mozzarella

Combine the cornmeal with the fresh corn. Add to this the peppers and jalapeño. Add a smidgen of baking soda, some salt and moisten with milk until a fairly think batter forms. Pour the batter into a hot frying pan and cook in the butter. Flip over and cover with a slice of cheese. Fold the *cachapa* in half and serve, with tomato salsa on the side.

Breton Galettes

Ingredients
2 cups / 340 g buckwheat flour
2 eggs
pinch of salt
2 tablespoons melted butter

In a large bowl mix together the buckwheat flour, eggs, a good pinch of salt, the melted butter and enough cold water to make a thin batter. Mix this with your hand, aerating the batter with violent slapping motions, as if punishing it. Continue until all your frustrations have abated and flecks of brown batter are scattered all over the kitchen. Cook the galettes on a hot non-stick crêpe pan or large frying pan, the thinner the better. Top them with something savoury such as mushrooms in a béchamel sauce, ham and cheese or, best of all, shellfish in a light cream sauce. Fold each corner of the galette over so you have a square shape with a little window in the centre revealing the contents. Serve with icy cold dry cider.

Crêpes Poseidon

Ingredients
1 cup / 125 g flour
⅔ cup / 155 ml milk
⅔ cup / 150 ml water
3 eggs
3 tablespoons melted butter
pinch of salt
1 shallot, minced
butter for frying
1 cup / 130 g shelled shrimp
1 cup / 135 g crabmeat
1 cup or handful scallops
pinch of tarragon

a few saffron threads
¼ cup / 55 ml dry white wine
¼ cup / 55 ml heavy cream

Mix the flour with the milk, water, eggs, butter and salt. Let the mixture rest for at least an hour in the refrigerator, adding more water if necessary to make a thin batter. Heat a shallow crêpe pan or frying pan, add a little butter and ladle in some batter, swirling it around to cover the pan and pouring the excess back into the mixing bowl. Flip and cook the other side a few seconds. Stack the crêpes as they are made and cover to keep warm. When done, gently cook the shallot in a tablespoon of butter without browning. Next add the shelled shrimp, crabmeat, scallops, tarragon and saffron. Cook gently for a minute or so, then add the dry white wine and cream, and reduce on high heat for a minute, letting the shellfish cook through. Fill the crêpes with the seafood and garnish with some seaweed, and a trident.

Palacsinta

Ingredients
6 eggs
3 cups / 375 g flour
1 ½ cups / 355 ml milk
1 tablespoon sugar
pinch of salt
1 ½ cups / 340 ml soda water
butter for frying
¼ cups / 30 g ground walnuts
a little honey
apricot jam
sweetened whipped cream for decoration

Make a crêpe-like batter by mixing together the eggs, flour, milk, sugar and a pinch of salt. Let the batter rest for several hours or overnight and then add the soda water. Make the crêpes as in the previous recipe and set aside. Stack the crêpes, separating each with the ground walnuts held together with a little honey, and alternate layers with apricot jam. Continue until all the crêpes are used and you have a 'cake' which can be decorated with piped sweetened whipped cream.

Latkes

Ingredients
3 potatoes, peeled and roughly chopped
1 onion
1 egg
pinch of salt
matzoh meal (enough to make a thick batter)
oil

Put into a blender the potatoes, onion, egg and a pinch of salt. Blend until smooth. Place the mixture in a strainer and let the liquid drain off for a few minutes. Discard the liquid. Put the remaining mixture in a bowl and add matzoh meal, about half the volume of the potato mixture, until a thick batter forms. Drop this by spoonfuls into hot oil in a deep frying pan and fry on both sides until golden brown. Sprinkle with salt. Serve immediately, or sooner, with some sour cream and apple sauce.

Blini

Ingredients
2 cups / 240 g buckwheat flour
1 tablespoon baking powder
2 eggs
milk (enough to make a thick pancake batter)
butter for frying
sour cream to taste
osetra caviar (the best you can afford)

Mix together the flour, baking powder, eggs and milk. Pour into a hot buttered frying pan or griddle to make small bite-size pancakes. Add a dollop of sour cream to each and top with the caviar. Serve with ice cold vodka, and make a toast to Tsar Nicholas.

Crêpes Suzette

Ingredients
4 cups / 500g flour, sifted
1 ½ cups / 200 g icing (powdered) sugar
pinch of fine salt
12 eggs
1.5 litres milk
2 tbsp curaçao
juice and zest of one mandarin orange
3 tbsp / 50g butter
¼ cup / 50g sugar

Mix the flour, sugar and salt in a bowl. Beat together the eggs and mix into the flour mixture, adding the milk little by little until you have a batter.

Perfume with a tablespoon of curacao and one of mandarin juice. Make the crêpes very thinly. Spread the butter and sugar on them. Add, working into the mixture with a spatula, the rest of the mandarin juice, together with its zest, and the second spoonful of curaçao. Once the mixture has covered all the crêpes, fold them into quarters and serve them flambéed.

Select Bibliography

Ahmed, Anne, ed., *A Proper Newe Booke of Cokerye* (Cambridge, 2002)

Ashkenazi, Michael and Jeanne Jacob, *Food Culture in Japan* (Westport, CT, 2003)

Atkinson, Lucy, *Recollections of Tartar Steppes and Their Inhabitants* (London, 1863)

Aunt Babbette's Cookbook (Cincinnati, OH, 1889); on Feeding America site: digital.lib.msu/projects/cookbooks/html/authors/author_aunt/html

Austin, Thomas, ed., *Two Fifteenth Century Cookbooks* (Rochester, NY, 2000 reprint)

Brattpfanne, Göttfried, *Das Ursprung des Eierkuchensänger und Waffelungenlieder* (Frankfurt am Main, 1897)

Carême, Marie Antonin, *L'Art de la cuisine française*, facsimile reprint of 1844 edn (Boston, MA, 2005)

Catholicon Anglicum (1483; London, Early English Text Society, 1999)

Child, Lydia Maria, *The Frugal American Housewife*, facsimile reprint of 1844 edn, intro. Janice Bluestein Longone (Minneola, NY, 1996)

Dalby, Andrew, *Food in the Ancient World from A–Z* (London, 2003)

Dawson, Thomas, *The Good Housewife's Jewel*, intro. Maggie Black (Lewes, 1996)

Dekker, Thomas, 'The Shoemaker's Holiday' in *The Roaring Girl* and Other City Comedies (Oxford, 2001)

Drake, Nathan, *Shakespeare and His Times* (Paris, 1843)

Ellis, William, *The Country Housewife's Family Companion*, reprint of
1750 edn, intro. Malcolm Thick (Totnes, 2000)

Fisher, Abby, *What Mrs. Fisher Knows About Southern Cooking*, facsimile reprint of 1881 edn, notes Karen Hess (Bedford, MA,
1995)

Francatelli, Charles Elmé, *A Plain Cookery Book for the Working
Classes*, facsimile reprint of 1861 edn (Whitstable, 1993)

Galen of Pergamum, *Galen on Food and Diet*, trans. Mark Grant
(London, 2000)

—, *On the Properties of Foodstuffs*, trans. Owen Powell (Cambridge,
2003)

Glasse, Hannah, *The Art of Cookery Made Plain and Easy*, facsimile
reprint of 1805 edn, ed. Karen Hess (Bedford, MA, 1997)

The Good Huswifes Handmaide for the Kitchen ([1594?] Bristol, 1992)

Grockock, Christopher and Sally Grainger, trans, *Apicius* (Totnes,
2006)

Hale, Sarah Josepha, *Early American Cookery*, facsimile reprint of
The Good Housekeeper, 1841, intro. Janice Bluestein Longone
(Minneola, NY, 1996)

Heiatt, Constance B. and Sharon Butler, eds, *Curye on Inglysch:
English Culinary Manuscripts of the Fourteenth Century (Including
the Forme of Cury)* (Oxford, 1985)

Hone, William, *The Yearbook of Daily Recreations* (London, 1839)

Hugget, Jane, ed., *A Proper Newe Booke of Cokerye*, transcript of an
anonymous mid-sixteenth century cookery book (Bristol,
1995)

Kettilby, Mary, *A Collection Above Three Hundred Receipts in Cookery*,
4th edn (London, 1728)

Leslie, Eliza, *Directions for Cookery* (Philadelphia, PA, 1840)

Liber de coquina; online at www.uni-giessen.de/gloning/tx/
mul2-lib.html; from Marianne Mulon, 'Deux traits inédits
d'art culinaire medieval', *Bulletin philologique et historique
(jusqu'au 1610) du Comité des Travaux historiques et scientifiques 1968*,
vol. 1 (1971)

Livre fort excellent de cuisine (Lyon, 1555)

Manring, M. M., *Slave in a Box: The Strange Career of Aunt Jemima* (Charlottesville, VA, 1998)

Markham, Gervase, *The English Housewife*, ed. Michael R. Best ([1625] Montreal, 1986)

Marnettè, Mounsieur (*sic*), *The Perfect Cook*, trans. of *Le Patissier François* by de La Varenne (London, 1656)

Mason, Charlotte, *The Lady's Assistant*, 2nd edn (London, 1775)

May, Robert, *The Accomplisht Cook*, reprint of 1685 edn (Totnes, 2000)

Le Menagier de Paris, The Goodman of Paris, trans. Eileen Power (London, 1992)

Notabel boecxken can cokeryen, Een (Brussels: Thomas van der Noot, 1514). http://users.pandora.be/willy.vancammeren/NBC/index.htm]]

Parloa, Maria, *Miss Parloa's New Cookbook* (1881); harvestfields.ca/CookBooks/001/01/000.htm

Pleij, Herman, *Dreaming of Cockaigne* (New York, 2001)

Randolf, Mary, *The Virginia House-wife*, facsimile of 1824 edn, commentary Karen Hess (Columbia, SC, 1984)

Simmons, Amelia, *American Cookery*, facsimile of 2nd edn, intro. Karen Hess (Bedford, MA, 1996)

—, *The First American Cookbook*, facsimile of *American Cookery*, 1796, intro. Mary Tolford Wilson (Minneola, NY, 1984)

Smith, E., *The Compleat Housewife*, first pub. 1758 (London, 1994)

Soyer, Alexis, *Shilling Cookery for the People*, facsimile reprint of 1860 edn (Whitstable, 1999)

Taylor, John, *Jack-a-Lent* (London, 1620)

De Verstandige Kock (Amsterdam, 1667); trans. as *The Sensible Cook* by Peter G. Rose (Syracuse, NY, 1989)

Websites and Associations

Olney Pancake Race
www.sideburn.demon.co.uk/olney/pancake.html

Shrove Tuesday
www.pancakeparlour.com/Annual_Events/Shrove/
shrove.html

Crepes
whatscookingamerica.net/History/CrepesSuzetteHistory.htm

Aunt Jemima
www.auntjemima.com/

Pancake Appreciation Society
www.welovepancakes.com/history/

Pancake History

Clabber Girl
www.clabbergirl.com/familyfun-Pancakes.php

Food Site
www.foodsiteoftheday.com/pancakes2.htm

The Pancake: An Appreciation

www.restaurantbiz.com/index.php?option=com_
content&task=view&id=13259&Itemid=93

Pancake Houses

International House of Pancakes
www.ihop.com/

The Original Pancake House
www.originalpancakehouse.com/

Perkins Restaurant and Bakery
www.perkinsrestaurants.com/history.html

Pancake Recipes

Epicurian.com
pancake-recipes.epicurean.com/asc_results.jsp?
title=Pancake

Epicurious.com
www.epicurious.com/tools/searchresults?search=pancakes

Pancake Recipes.com
www.pancakes-recipes.com/

Suite 101
www.suite101.com/reference/pancakes

Pancake Art

Web Gallery of Art (Search term: pancake)
www.wga.hu/index1.html

Pancake Music Videos

Pancakes!
www.youtube.com/watch?v=PNCVZOZHTG8

Pancakes II: Pancakes For Your Face
www.youtube.com/watch?v=UG5go4nlLRQ

Acknowledgements

In composing this essay I received the kind and gracious assistance of many souls who sent me recipes, lent me pans and egged me on with their encouragement for what would otherwise have seemed like an odd way to spend part of a sabbatical. I first thank Andy Smith, who roped me into doing this project, knowing full well that I am chasing his publication record and couldn't refuse. He said, 'Hey, want to write a book on something fun?' Without any deliberation whatsoever I replied, 'Sure, how about pancakes?' That was it. I must also thank the few people who found out I was doing this and helped: my former student, George Yagi, who pointed out the brilliant pancake passages in Ellis; my colleague, Wild Bill Swagerty, who lent me books and told me about Old Pancake Comstock; my former Dean, Bob Cox, who mused over Middle English *opacum*; the Foleys for a lovely *palacsinta barackízzel* recipe; Sandy Cooperman who lent me a munk pan and gave me her mother's *aebleskiver* recipe; my pal William Rubel who sent me electronic cookbooks from which I gleaned many pancake crumbs. Thanks to my boys E-bone and Mookie, and my wife, who actually ate some of these pancakes. A great big juicy thanks to Nancy Ellen Jones who came to my house to shoot every pancake I could cook in a single raucous day, and to my old pal Chris Martin, who set this up and served as key grip, assistant stylist and gourmand at large. Among these pancakes were some indescribably delicious *bánh xèo* prepared by Chun Sokhan Y through the agency of her daughter, Callyan, one of my favourite students.

Photo Acknowledgements

The author and publishers wish to express their thanks to the below sources of illustrative material and/or permission to reproduce it. Some locations of artworks are also supplied here.

Photo author: p. 51; photo © Carmen Martinez Banús/2008 iStock International Inc.: p. 91; photo John Collier/Library of Congress, Washington, DC (Prints and Photographs Division): p. 86; photo Paul Cowan/BigStockPhoto: p. 81; photo © Dobri Dobrinov/2008 iStock International Inc.: p. 102; photos Everett Collection/courtesy of Rex Features: pp. 45, 47, 49; photos Mitiku Gabrehiwot, courtesy Tania Tribe: p. 58; Haarlem Museum: p. 71; photo © Albert Harlingue/Roger-Viollet/Rex Features: p. 32; photo William F. Holmes: p. 100; photo © LAPI/Roger-Viollet/Rex Features: p. 76; photos Michael Leaman/Reaktion Books: pp. 53, 55, 56, 61; photos courtesy of the Library of Congress, Washington, DC (Prints and Photographs Division): pp. 21, 36; photo © ND/Roger-Viollet/Rex Features: p. 26; photo © Sandra O'Claire/2008 iStock International Inc.: p. 11; Philadelphia Museum of Art (John G. Johnson Collection): p. 31 (Brouwer, *The Pancake Baker*); photo Jonathan Player/Rex Features: p. 92; photo © Hazel Proudlove/2008 iStock International Inc.: p. 6; photo Geoff Robinson/Rex Features: pp. 66–7; photos © Roger-Viollet/Rex Features: pp. 15, 35 (van Brekelenkam, *Woman Tossing Crepes*), 71, 85 (Moulinet, *The Crepes*), 93; photos © Wisconsin Historical

Society/Everett Collection/Rex Features: pp. 38, 87; photo ©
Lisa F. Young/2008 iStock International Inc.: p. 72.

For pp. 8, 13, 16, 17, 37, 39, 59, 73, 77, 79, 83, 95, 98:

Nancy Ellen Jones: Photography and Food Styling
Chris Martin: Key Grip and Styling Assistant
Ken Albala: Food Preparation
Ken and Joanna Albala: Pottery

Shot on location in Stockton, California

Index

italic numbers refer to illustrations; **bold** to recipes